NEBS
MANAGEMENT
DEVELOPMENT

SUPER SERIES

THIRD EDITION
Managing People

Managing
Lawfully

– People and
Employment

Published for

 &NEBS Management *by*

 **Pergamon Open Learning**

Pergamon Open Learning
An imprint of Butterworth-Heinemann
Linacre House, Jordan Hill, Oxford OX2 8DP
A division of Reed Educational and Professional Publishing Ltd

ℛ A member of the Reed Elsevier plc group

OXFORD BOSTON JOHANNESBURG
MELBOURNE NEW DELHI SINGAPORE

First published 1986
Second edition 1991
Third edition 1997

British Library Cataloguing in Publication Data
A catalogue record for this book is available from the British Library

ISBN 0 7506 3320 4

The author acknowledges the following organization for
their kind permission to allow reproduction of
copyright material: ACAS (*Employment Handbook,
Discipline at Work*).

The views expressed in this work are those
of the authors and do not necessarily reflect
those of the National Examining Board for
Supervision and Management or of the publisher.

NEBS Management Project Manager: Diana Thomas
Author: Angus Thomas
Editor: Ian Bloor
Series Editor: Diana Thomas
Based on previous material by: Joe Johnson
Composition by Genesis Typesetting, Rochester, Kent
Printed and bound in Great Britain

Contents

Workbook introduction

1 NEBS Management Super Series 3 study links

Here are the workbook titles in each module which link with *Managing Lawfully – People and Employment*, should you wish to extend your study to other Super Series workbooks. There is a brief description of each workbook in the User Guide.

This workbook is based upon legislation which applies in England and Wales. Although much of the legislation referred to also applies in Scotland you should bear in mind that Scotland has its own legal system, legal traditions and system of courts and tribunals. We have not attempted to take into account specific matters of Scottish law in this workbook.

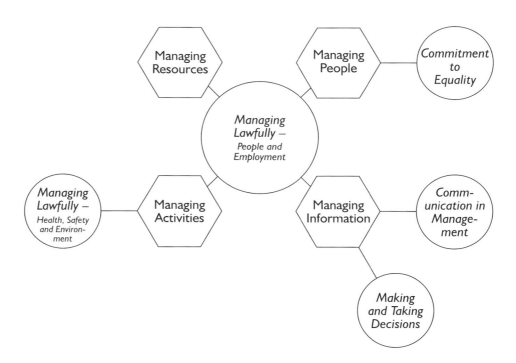

2 S/NVQ links

This workbook relates to the following elements:

C15.2 Contribute to implementing disciplinary and grievance procedures

It is designed to help you to develop the following Personal Competences:

- thinking and taking decisions;
- building teams;
- focusing on results;
- striving for excellence.

3 Workbook objectives

Our work is, whether we really enjoy it or not, one of the most important things in our lives. Very few of us are sufficiently wealthy that we do not depend on our salary in order to provide all the things that we need. This is one of the main reasons why employment law is so important. We all need to know what our contracts mean, what legal rights we have in work and how we should be treated if we are ever disciplined at work, or even dismissed.

Work is as important for the people whom you supervise as it is for everyone else. Their security depends on you treating them properly which means that you must understand, and act in accordance with, employment law.

Because work is so important, many people choose to join trade unions in order to gain extra protection for themselves. In this workbook, we will look at trade unions in the workplace and the ways in which they can work with front line managers.

We will also look at all of the stages of employment, from the forming of a contract of employment to disciplinary action and dismissal. It's important to note that, through each of these stages, the law is there to ensure that both employer and employee act reasonably and responsibly towards each other.

Remember that a knowledge of employment law is important but we must not overlook the fact that employment depends on relationships between people. We should aim to improve those relationships, rather than damage them through imposing unnecessary punishments and penalties.

3.1 Objectives

When you have worked through this workbook you will be better able to:

- explain what a contract of employment is, and what should be contained in a written statement of terms and conditions;
- understand, and work effectively with, trade union representatives;
- deal with disciplinary problems in a fair and consistent way;
- explain the law relating to dismissal.

4 Activity planner

The following Activities require some planning so you may want to look at these now.

- For Activity 19 you are asked to explain:
  - how well you ensure that your team members are kept informed of the organization's disciplinary procedures;
  - the actions you intend to take to make them better informed;
  - how confident you are that the contributions you make to implementing disciplinary and grievance procedures are consistent with your organization's values and policies;
  - and, if you are less than totally confident about this, what actions you will take.

- Activity 28 asks some self-searching questions about whether you and your colleagues are consistent in treating individuals with respect, and keep disciplinary matters confidential.

- In Activity 35 a number of questions are asked regarding your disciplinary records.

Portfolio of evidence

Some or all of these Activities may provide the basis of evidence for your S/NVQ portfolio. All Portfolio Activities and the Work-based assignment are signposted with this icon.

The icon states the elements to which the Portfolio Activities and Work-based assignment relate.

Session A Contracts of employment

1 Introduction

A contract is simply an agreement. Contracts are made when one party agrees what he or she will each do in return for the actions of another. The father who agrees to give his son an extra 50p pocket money each week so long as the son keeps his bedroom tidy enters into a contract, albeit a very simple one. The father and son are both promising to do something in return for the actions of the other.

In the area of employment, contracts are important and necessary. They spell out the promises made on both sides, which is very useful in case of a subsequent disagreement. Employees, for example, are able to go to court and demand compensation if they have stuck to their side of the bargain and their employer has not.

Another advantage of a contract is that it helps to make clear what each party's commitments are, and to prevent abuses. An employee being asked to work twice as many hours for half as much pay as previously would look to his or her contract, and to employment law, for protection against an overwhelming workload.

In this session we will examine how a contract is formed and the things that it should include.

2 The contract

A contract of employment is key to any agreement to work or employ.

Activity 1

2 mins

■ Lettie Jarvis wanted a cleaner to work after hours to clean and tidy her shop. She advertised in the local paper and eventually decided to offer the job to Molly Hemsley. Lettie showed the work area to Molly and explained what she wanted done. Then she told Molly the wages she was prepared to offer, and asked her when she could start. Molly agreed to start work the following day.

Molly is going to work for Lettie. Based on their discussion, do you think that a contract of employment exists between the pair? Explain your reasoning, briefly.

_____

_____

_____

_____

In fact, a contract of employment does exist, even though there is nothing in writing, and even if Lettie and Molly didn't shake hands on the agreement. As soon as Molly accepted the terms and conditions of the job that were offered, the contract came into effect.

Later, Lettie, not being used to employing people, wondered whether the contract was legal and whether she would have to put something in writing.

A contract of employment does not have to be in writing. However, all employees are entitled to a **written statement of the main terms and conditions of employment**.

Under the Employment Protection (Consolidation) Act 1978, as amended by the Trade Union Reform and Employment Rights Act 1993, they must receive this within eight weeks of starting work.

What should be in this written statement?

Activity 2

What points about a contract of employment would you expect to find in the written statement? One thing you might expect to find is the hours of work. Try to list **three** other things.

_____

_____

_____

_____

EXTENSION I
Details of this handbook are given on page 75.

The ACAS (Advisory, Conciliation and Arbitration Service) *Employment Handbook* lists the following points of information, which should be included in the written statement of the main terms and conditions of employment:

Employees who are employed for less than one month do not have a statutory right to a written statement.

- the employer's name;
- the place of work and the address of the employer;
- the employee's name;
- the date employment began;
- the date on which the employee's period of continuous employment began (taking into account any employment with a previous employer which counts towards that period);
- where the period is not permanent, the period it is expected to continue;
- where the employment is for a fixed term, the date when it is to end;
- the job title;
- the amount of pay and the interval between payments;
- hours of work;
- holiday pay and entitlement;
- sickness and sick pay arrangements;
- pensions;
- whether a contracting-out certificate under the Social Security Act 1975 is in force;
- notice periods;
- a note specifying any disciplinary rules and to whom employees can apply if they are dissatisfied with a disciplinary decision;
- a note on grievance procedures specifying to whom employees can apply to seek redress of any grievance;
- any collective agreements which directly affect the terms and conditions;
- where a person is required to work outside the UK for more than one month, the period he/she is to do so; the terms and conditions relating to his/her return to the UK.

Employers with fewer than 20 employees are exempt from the requirement to provide employees with a note on disciplinary rules, but should provide details of the person to whom an employee can express a grievance.

The written statement must set out the employee's terms and conditions in full. It is not sufficient to refer employees to some other document, such as a collective agreement or a staff handbook. There are, however, three exceptions to this rule. The written statement can refer the employee to some other document for detailed information on:

■ particulars of sick pay terms;
■ particulars of pension entitlements;
■ terms relating to notice of termination of the contract (i.e. relevant statutory provisions or a collective agreement).

Of course, if there is a written contract it can include reference to other matters, not mentioned above, which have been agreed. For instance, a contract might state that:

■ everyone can be searched by security staff;
■ all management staff can be expected to move to another work location should the need ever arise;
■ managers must not profit from their involvement with the organization after they leave, or must not allow future employers to profit from this involvement.

2.1 Terms of a contract

There are four main categories of terms in a contract of employment. These are known as:

■ express terms;
■ implied terms;
■ incorporated terms;
■ statutory terms.

Let's look at each of these.

■ Express terms

All the terms that are explained clearly and in detail in a contract (whether the contract is in writing or there is simply a spoken agreement) are called the **express terms**.

■ Implied terms

Terms that are too obvious to mention, or which are not stated because they are accepted custom and practice in the kind of work being done, are called **implied terms**. For instance, there are certain implied obligations on an employee.

Activity 3

Try to think of an implied obligation on the part of you and your workteam, which probably isn't a specific item in your contracts of employment. For instance, one implied obligation is to be honest.

_____

_____

Some implied obligations are:

■ to exercise reasonable skill and care in doing your job;
■ to be honest in your dealings with people;
■ to take care of an employer's property;
■ to be loyal to your employer (such as refusing to provide a competitor with company confidential information);
■ to obey reasonable instructions.

There are implied terms imposed on the employer, too. These include being obliged to:

■ treat employees with reasonable courtesy and consideration;
■ provide reasonable support to enable employees to do their work;
■ provide a safe work environment.

You will notice that the word **reasonable** occurs in both the lists above. This is a word that crops up quite often in employment law. What is reasonable can only be ultimately decided in a court of law. Fortunately, for most of the time, people agree between themselves about what is reasonable.

■ Incorporated terms

If an employer recognizes a trade union, the employer and union may agree that employees' terms and conditions can be negotiated between them through a process called **collective bargaining**.

In this case, an individual's contract of employment may include references to the collective bargaining agreement.

Terms such as this in a contract of employment, which incorporate terms from other documents, are called **incorporated terms**.

In the next Session we will look in more detail at collective bargaining.

■ Statutory terms

Statutory terms are those imposed by law.

Activity 4

3 mins

■ Darlene Lester was ambitious and was convinced that she deserved promotion in her job. She felt that she was being held back from making progress because she was a woman, and all the senior positions were held by men. Darlene decided to read her contract of employment carefully and was rather upset to find that it made no specific reference to discrimination. She wondered if her employer could 'get away' with discriminating against her because she had agreed the terms and conditions when she joined.

Did Darlene have cause to be concerned? Could the contract of employment take away her rights not to be discriminated against? Jot down your views on this case.

_____

_____

_____

_____

There is a clear answer here. No contract can take away someone's legal rights. There are various laws which exist to prevent discrimination in employment. Protection exists against discrimination on the grounds of sex, marriage, race, colour, nationality, ethnic origin, national origins and disability. These laws apply whatever any contract of employment says or fails to say.

It is important to note that whereas a contract can give an employee more rights than are specified by law, it cannot give less. Employees cannot sign away their legal rights.

Now let's move on to consider what happens when a contract is changed.

3 Changing the contract

Changes to a contract of employment should normally only be made if both the employer and the employee agree. In some cases, an employee might wish to take advice from his or her trade union about agreeing to proposed changes in their contract.

The likelihood is that you have already agreed a change in your contract with your present employer.

Activity 5

Can you think of **two** kinds of changes to a contract which could be agreed between employer and employee?

_____

_____

You may have suggested one or more of the following:

- a promotion;
- a pay rise;
- a move to a new location;
- an increase in holiday entitlement.

If a proposed change affects anything which is in an employee's written statement of the main terms and conditions of employment then notice of the change must be given in writing.

What if the employer changes the terms and conditions of employment **without** the employee's consent? In this case, there is a **breach of contract**.

> An Industrial Tribunal is a board appointed to handle legal disputes such as those of alleged unfair dismissal.

If an employee's contract has been breached then it is up to that person to take action. If they do not object to a change in their contract of which they are aware then, after a 'significant period', the employer can claim that the employee, by continuing to work without objection, has given their implied consent. There are no clear guidelines on what is meant here by 'a significant period', but the time limit for complaints to an Industrial Tribunal in this case is three months.

- Mr Clements, who had been a first line manager in a factory for ten years, had been paid his wages every week for the whole of that time. One pay day the wages arrived but there was a £10 shortfall. Mr Clements was informed by his employer that in future he would receive £10 less than had been agreed in his pay packet each week.

> ACAS advises that if there are changes to any of the terms and conditions set out in the written statement, the employer must give the employee a new written statement within a month of the change.

If he wasn't prepared to accept the reduction in pay, Mr Clements had two courses open to him. He could either:

- claim damages for breach of contract in a court of law; or
- resign, and claim 'constructive dismissal' at an Industrial Tribunal.

We'll take a look at constructive dismissal later, in Session D.

Of course, an employee might break a contract, as the following case illustrates.

- Mrs Greenaway, a sales supervisor, left fourteen vacuum cleaners belonging to her employer in a car outside her house one night, and they were stolen. Her employer was entitled to claim compensation from Mrs Greenaway because she had failed in her duty to exercise reasonable care in doing her job. This is an **implied term** of almost all contracts of employment.

In summary, a contract of employment is much like any other kind of contract. Before it's altered in any way, both parties to the contract should agree. If one side breaks the contract, then the other side may be entitled to compensation or to take some other action. In practice of course, employers rarely try to claim compensation; however, they may well have good grounds for terminating the contract.

4 Terminating the contract

A contract of employment can be terminated if

- both employer and employee agree to do so;
- either the employer or the employee gives the other party the required notice.

If an employee is guilty of 'gross misconduct', he or she can be dismissed without notice. We'll take a closer look at this in Session D.

4.1 Periods of notice

All employees are entitled to at least:

- one week's notice after one month's service;
- two weeks' notice after two years; and
- an extra one week's notice for every year of employment up to a maximum of 12 weeks for 12 years of service.

An employee only has to give one week's notice after one month's service, and this doesn't increase with longer service.

These periods of notice can be longer if this has been agreed in the contract of employment.

Employees may agree to accept pay instead of working out a notice.

Self-assessment 1

6 mins

1   Can a contract of employment exist if nothing has been written down? Give a brief reason for your answer.

_____

Fill the blanks in the following sentences.

2   All employees are entitled to get a statement, which spells out the main terms and conditions of their employment, within _____ _____ of starting work.

3   Once an employee agrees to the terms in a contract of employment, he or she must abide by them, or be guilty of _____ .

4   As an employee, you are obliged to take reasonable care in the way you do your job, even if it doesn't say so in your contract. This is an _____ _____ in your contract.

5   If a contract of employment incorporates a collective bargaining agreement, the terms of the contract can be changed without the express approval of the employee. This is known as an _____ term.

6   A _____ _____ _____ occurs when an employer changes the terms of a contract without the consent of the employee.

Answers to these questions can be found on page 82.

5 Summary

- A **contract of employment** exists as soon as the employee accepts the terms and conditions of the job offered by the employer.

- All employees are entitled to a **written statement of the main terms and conditions of employment**.

- All the terms which are explained clearly and in detail in a contract are called the **express terms**.

- Terms which are too obvious to mention, or which are not stated because they are accepted custom and practice in the kind of work being done, are called **implied terms**.

- Terms such as this in a contract of employment, which incorporate terms from other documents, are called **incorporated terms**.

- **Statutory terms** are those which are imposed by law.

- Changes to a contract of employment should normally only be made if both the employer and the employee agree.

- A contract of employment can be terminated if:

  - both employer and employee agree to do so;
  - either the employer or the employee gives the other party the required notice.

- A contract of employment can also be terminated if an employer has grounds to dismiss an employee.

Session B Working with trade unions

1 Introduction

Why do individuals form themselves into groups? There are almost as many possible answers to this question as there are clubs, associations and teams. However, there are some reasons which apply in almost all cases. These reasons include:

- working toward common goals;
- sharing information;
- using a collective strength that individuals do not have alone;
- joining together for protection.

If you have a car you may be a member of an organization providing a breakdown service, such as the Automobile Association or the Royal Automobile Club. People join those groups for protection. You might be a member of an organization such as the National Trust. In that case there is a common goal – the preservation and enjoyment of beautiful buildings, gardens and parklands.

These same reasons are what drive people to join trade unions. You may be a trade union member yourself. The primary purpose of trade unions has always been to represent people in work. This involves negotiating on their behalf and working to ensure that they are not treated unfairly.

You are likely to have some contact with trade unions and their members through your work. As a team leader you may be called upon to negotiate with union representatives. This Session is intended to help you in that important role.

We will examine the way in which trade unions are organized, look at the role that you may play in dealing with trade unions and see how, and why, unions can become involved in your team-leading work.

It is important to remember that trade unions are there to represent workers in your organization. The employees who choose to be represented by unions are vital to your organization's success, whatever kind of business you might be involved in. Almost always, co-operation between managers and union representatives will serve both groups better than will confrontation. As we shall see, you can often benefit from the involvement of trade unions in the workplace.

Let's start by answering some questions about trade unions.

11

2 Trade unions – an overview

Often, trade unions are portrayed as old-fashioned groups for manual workers in cloth caps. It also often seems that the main activity of trade unions is the organizing of strikes. Neither of these images reflects the work of modern trade unions.

Activity 6

3 mins

Try to answer the following questions.

■ What kind of people are members of trade unions?

_____

■ For whose benefit do trade unions exist?

_____

■ Does a union represent individuals or whole groups?

_____

See whether you agree to the following answers to these questions.

■ Employees are members of trade unions.
■ A union exists for the benefit of its members.
■ A union represents both individuals and groups.

3 The structure of trade unions

Most trade unions are organized at three levels. These levels are:

■ the union branch level;
■ an intermediate level;
■ the delegate conference.

The **union branch** is the level which is 'closest to home'. The branches are where ordinary members of the union meet and have an opportunity to express their views.

The branch is the lowest level of trade union structure; it is also often the most important. In most representative organizations decision making both begins and ends with members of the branches.

Trade union branches come in three forms:

- The first is workplace branches which are made up of all union members in one particular workplace.
- The second is geographical branches which are made up of all members in a particular geographical area.
- The third form is called a mixed branch. This is a combination of the other two forms. An example would be a company which has two or three sites in a big city. The branch would then cover all members of the union at these sites.

Most unions, like most other large organizations, have an **intermediate level**. The groups at this level have different titles in different unions. They may be described as 'Districts', 'Divisions', 'Regions' or 'Areas'. Whatever title might be given, the intermediate level has an important administrative role to play.

It is at the intermediate level that disputes within or between branches are often resolved. Also, much of the trade union policy-making process is often carried out at this intermediate level.

The highest stage within the structure of trade unions is the **delegate conference**. These conferences usually take place annually. Delegates from branches come together in order to finally decide union policies and to elect a National Executive Committee. This committee is charged with administering and controlling the union between conferences, with implementing the union's policies and with representing the union's membership in negotiations and to the media.

It's important that you know how unions are put together but we shall now turn to the level you are most likely to deal with. The key figure in the workplace is the **shop steward**.

4 The shop steward

What is a shop steward?

A shop steward is someone who is acceptable to both management and union as a representative of trade union members at his or her own workplace.

He or she has responsibility for the initial stages of negotiations in the workplace.

The shop steward is not a full-time official of the union.

As a team leader you are likely to deal with shop stewards directly if your workplace is one in which unions are active. Indeed, you may be a shop steward yourself.

Other titles may be used instead of 'shop steward'. In the printing trade they are often known as fathers, or mothers, of the chapel. For white-collar workers they are often known as the office representative (rep).

The first line manager and the shop steward have much in common. For one thing, both have a great deal to contribute to the organization and its employees.

Activity 7

3 mins

Can you think of something else that a shop steward and a first line manager have in common?

_____

_____

_____

_____

As you may have observed, first line managers and shop stewards are both representatives of employees and have responsibilities towards them.

A first line manager is a representative of the workteam in dealings with higher management. A shop steward is a representative of union members in dealings with management.

Crucially, both the first line manager and the shop steward have it in their power to improve relationships in the workplace or to destroy them.

A shop steward's job is not easy. He or she really has three separate roles. A shop steward is:

■ an employee, with a job to do; the company has a right to expect loyalty and 'a fair day's work for a fair day's pay' from the shop steward, as from any other employee;
■ a representative of the individual in discussions with management about grievances and so on;
■ a representative of a group in collective negotiations.

It is very important that first line managers and shop stewards are able to effectively work together. Members of a union deserve to have their views represented properly and an employer will suffer eventually if the first line manager's role as communicator with shop stewards is not properly being carried out.

Occasionally, conflicts between first line managers and shop stewards can arise, as they can between any people who are working together.

Activity 8

3 mins

Have you ever felt that a shop steward was undermining your authority? If so, what did you do about it?

_____

_____

_____

_____

It is not unknown for a first line manager to feel that a shop steward was, to some extent, undermining his or her authority.

There may be an occasion when your workteam members feel that their interests are best served by supporting an action by a shop steward, even though you may feel that this action is contrary to your own objectives.

Your own position depends on two things:

- the backing you receive from management in your dealings with representatives;
- the integrity and honesty you display in your dealings with people.

You need the backing of management because without it you are fighting a losing battle. However, I hope you agree that if your team members see that you have their interests at heart, as well as those of the organization, and that you are honestly trying your best to get a job done, you are likely to retain their respect.

The relationship between the shop steward and the first line manager is a vital one in industrial relations. Each should recognize the need to keep the other informed of grievances, plans and problems.

Mutual co-operation brings mutual respect.

5 Collective bargaining

In many areas, trade unions represent their members through a process called **collective bargaining**.

A collective bargaining arrangement is a procedure whereby employers and employee representatives agree to negotiate matters, such as pay and conditions of service, on a group basis for the employees in a particular company or industry.

Remember, a collective bargaining agreement could be one of the incorporated terms of a contract of employment which we discussed in Session A.

Around 40 per cent of the employees in this country have their wages, terms and conditions of employment determined by collective bargaining.

Activity 9

6 mins

Why might employees wish to be represented through collective bargaining?

_____

_____

_____

_____

There are a number of possible reasons why employees might favour collective bargaining. Here are two of the main ones:

- Union negotiators are well versed in employment law. They can ensure that a deal which is struck is both legal and fair.
- Some employees are not as confident as others. People don't want to lose out compared to their colleagues because they couldn't argue as effectively.

Activity 10

3 mins

Why might employers wish to negotiate through collective bargaining?

_____

_____

_____

_____

Again, there are many possible reasons. The main ones in this case are not that different from those we just looked at.

- Negotiating one collective deal is much more efficient than negotiating with a number of employees individually.
- Trade union negotiators are experienced. They understand the priorities of employers and the relevant laws.
- Collective bargaining ensures that all employees are treated equally. It avoids potentially disruptive divisions between employees.

Collective bargaining can, of course, only take place where employees are represented by a trade union or another representative body.

6 Union recognition

If some of the employees in an organization have joined a trade union, the union may make a request to the employer for **recognition**. This normally means that a formal agreement is drawn up between the two parties. Under this, the union gains the right to negotiate on its members' behalf.

Activity 11

4 mins

Note **two** reasons why an organization might decide to recognize a trade union.

_____

_____

_____

_____

There is a variety of reasons why an organization might recognize a union. Here are three reasons:

- because it already recognizes unions in another part of the organization;
- because there is considerable demand from employees and union membership is a substantial proportion of the workforce;
- because the organization needs a method of consulting and negotiating with staff and feels that the union will help to provide this.

Unions which do not represent a substantial proportion of the workforce might be granted representation rights rather than full recognition. Representation rights mean that the union is allowed to represent individuals in cases of discipline or grievance.

Once an employer has decided to recognize a trade union there are a number of rights which the recognized union gains.

These rights include:

- receiving certain kinds of information about the organization, where the union is recognized;
- being consulted before employees are made redundant;
- the power to appoint a safety representative;
- time off for its representatives for trade union activities and duties.

7 The scope of union involvement

Now let's look at a few practical situations which might arise at work.

Activity 12

Here are three situations which could easily arise at work. Read each of the following cases. In your opinion, are these situations ones in which a trade union might be helpful? If you think a union could help then write a brief description of what the union might do.

- Rachel Dosumnu has been asked to attend a meeting with her first line manger to discuss her poor work rate.

_____

How could a trade union help?

_____

_____

_____

- Dylan McNichol is working eight hours a day at a computer screen which is causing him to develop headaches and, he feels, is damaging his eyesight.

_____

How could a trade union help?

_____

_____

_____

■ Clive Elliot, a black man, is very unhappy at work because of racist remarks made by a few of the other workers.

How could a trade union help?

Here are some suggested ways in which a union could helpfully become involved in each of these cases:

■ Rachel Dosumnu's shop steward should make sure that she understands the organization's disciplinary procedures and knows what is likely to happen at the meeting. For reasons which we will look at in the next Session, it would be useful for Rachel to have her shop steward present at the meeting.
■ Dylan McNichol's shop steward should advise him about Health and Safety regulations, which require regular breaks from working at a computer screen. His union could raise the issue on his behalf. It could be that Dylan is not the only person who is suffering. It would strengthen Dylan's case enormously if the union could point to other members with similar difficulties.
■ Clive Elliot's position is very serious. The law forbids racial harassment at work. Employers who don't take complaints seriously can face large fines from Industrial Tribunals. The experience and knowledge of employment law which trade unions can bring to bear would help Clive a lot here. If informing his first line manager about the situation made no difference, Clive's trade union should be able to represent him at a tribunal.

In the next Session we'll look at how you might go about maintaining discipline in a workteam. There is also a role for shop stewards in that process, as we shall see.

Self-assessment 2

20 mins

1 Briefly describe the main function of trade unions.

2 What is collective bargaining?

3 Complete the following sentences.

■ When a trade union is granted _____ by an employer it gains the right to negotiate on behalf of its members, to receive certain kinds of information about the organization where it is organized, and to be consulted over redundancies.

■ When a union is granted _____ it gains the right to represent individuals in cases of discipline and grievance.

4 Which one of the following statements is **not** true?

a Shop stewards are full-time union officials.

b Trade unions represent individuals and groups.

c First line managers and shop stewards both represent employees.

Answers to these questions can be found on page 82.

8 Summary

■ The general aim of trade unions is to organize employees and to represent their interests.

■ A particular aim is to engage with employers in collective bargaining.

■ Unions are generally divided into branches and regions. A delegate conference decides union policies. A National Executive Committee runs the union between conferences.

■ A shop steward:

- is someone who is accepted by management and union as a representative of trade union members, at his or her own place of work;
- has responsibility for the initial stages of negotiations in the workplace;
- is not a full-time official of the union.

■ Collective bargaining is a procedure whereby employer and employee representatives agree to negotiate matters such as pay and conditions of service for the employees in a particular company or industry.

Session C Discipline

1 Introduction

Few organizations are as strict about discipline as an army. If soldiers were allowed to turn up at a battle at a time to suit themselves, and then could follow only the orders they chose to, the army wouldn't last long.

Of course, the army is an extreme example of discipline at work. It is unlikely that your workplace is run as strictly as a military camp! However, the reasons that discipline at work are important are very similar to the reasons why discipline is essential in a fighting force.

For a start, any group of people are much more effective when they work as a team. As a team leader in your own workplace you will no doubt appreciate that fact.

Without discipline, teamwork can easily break down. If individual members of a team are refusing to pull their weight, then the overall effectiveness of the group suffers. Other members, seeing that they are doing more than their colleagues, will either decide to take it easy themselves, or become angry that work is not being shared evenly.

Remember, discipline is not about punishment. It is about resolving problems at work in as fair a manner as possible. In the interests of fairness, there should always be clear rules about the way that disciplinary problems are dealt with. In this Session we'll examine each of those stages.

2 The purpose of discipline

This workbook concentrates on practical ways of handling discipline. However, before we start we should try to define what discipline is for.

Why does management make up sets of rules and penalize employees who don't conform to them?

Activity 13

Write down **two** purposes of discipline at work.

_____

_____

_____

_____

See whether you agree with the following arguments.

Discipline at work has four main objectives:

- safety;
- fairness;
- prosperity of the organization;
- compliance with a contract.

2.1 Safety

Someone entering a workplace for the first time won't necessarily be able to know how to behave. In particular, he or she probably won't be aware of the dangers of that workplace, and so won't be safe until told about the hazards and the means of protection against those hazards. Employees who ignore safety rules, or who indulge in fighting or drinking at work (for example) may endanger others.

2.2 Fairness

People who don't do as much as their colleagues, or who for instance take time off without good reason, are not being fair. Everyone has responsibilities at work; when someone shirks his or her responsibilities someone else has to take them up.

2.3 Prosperity of the organization

Any organization which employs people needs to get those people to work together in order to achieve its aims. If they are to work together successfully, people need to know what is expected of them. People who are incompetent, or who fail do to their job, cost their employers money which they can rarely afford.

2.4 Compliance with a contract

As we have already seen, a contract of employment is an agreement between an employer and an employee. One party gives wages and provides facilities and benefits: in exchange the other agrees to work to the best of his or her ability.

Discipline at work should work for the benefit of an organization and everyone who works in it.

And when dealing with a disciplinary offence, there is one guiding principle:

The main aim is improvement in performance, not punishment.

3 Rules

If there is to be discipline at work, there has to be a set of rules. Rules help to determine the standards of conduct expected from employees.

Because people need to know what is expected of them.

> **Everyone needs to know what the rules are, and the reasons for the rules.**

Activity 14

Note down **two** or **three** examples of the rules that affect the people at your place of work.

_____

_____

_____

Typical of the kinds of rules which are found in work organizations are:

- rules about timekeeping;
- rules about absence;
- rules about health and safety;
- rules about using company facilities;
- rules about who does what;
- rules about what constitutes gross misconduct.

Of course, the law of the land applies at work as well as outside it, even though the list of rules drawn up by an organization won't normally remind employees of that fact. It goes without saying that it is a disciplinary offence to steal or to damage property, for instance.

It's obviously preferable for the rules of an organization to be written down.

Activity 15

Even if the rules are written down, there can be problems in communicating the rules to all employees.

Note **one** such problem, and say how it could be overcome.

_____

_____

_____

_____

Problems can arise with:

- new employees, who aren't familiar with the accepted and safe ways to behave in that workplace. They need to have the rules **explained** to them – it usually isn't good enough simply to provide a copy of the rules, especially where safety is concerned. Explaining the rules forms part of an induction programme.
- people who don't speak English as their first language. The first line manager must take steps to **make sure** the rules are understood.
- young people, who don't have experience of working life. Again, it may fall to the first line manager to ensure that a young person **fully understands** the rules and why they have to be followed.

4 Dealing with offences

What is a disciplinary offence?

Activity 16

4 mins

Let's start by thinking about the disciplinary offences you may have had to deal with at work, or those you may have heard about.

Note down some examples of disciplinary offences. Try to think of **three** or **four**. An example is stealing.

_____

_____

_____

_____

Here are some disciplinary offences:

- fighting;
- verbal abuse;
- lateness;
- abusing company equipment;
- disobeying an instruction;
- stealing;
- smoking in a non-smoking area;
- horse-play.

You may have come up with offences not on this list. The list of disciplinary offences is as long as our imaginations can make it.

However, all these offences involve one thing:

all disciplinary offences involve a breach of rules.

If we want to deal with disciplinary offences in a consistent and fair way, we need to:

- know what the **rules** are; and
- have a well-designed **procedure** for dealing with people who break the rules.

Let's think about the steps a manager or team leader needs to take when there has been a suspected disciplinary offence.

25

Activity 17

3 mins

Suppose someone in another team stops you in the corridor and says something like:

'Two of your blokes left an hour early last night. That's not the first time. I don't think it's fair. What are you going to do about it?'

Well, what is the **first** thing you would do?

_____

_____

Perhaps you agree that the first thing to be done when a breach of the rules is reported is to:

find out the facts.

Until you've looked into the matter thoroughly to see if the accusation has any truth in it, you aren't in a position to judge.

Activity 18

3 mins

What might you do next, assuming you found out that **two** of your workteam had left early without permission?

_____

_____

You might do one of a number of things. You could for instance:

- have a quiet word with them;
- give them a warning about their behaviour;
- take the matter further and start formal disciplinary proceedings.

Any formal procedures usually involve a **disciplinary interview**. This gives the people accused a chance to state their version of the facts.

Then you would be able to come to a considered judgement about what penalty you should impose – if any.

Once you decided on the action to be taken, you'd need to record the information and keep an eye on things from that point on.

We can sum up all these steps in the form of a diagram. We'll be using this diagram as we go through the rest of this part of the workbook.

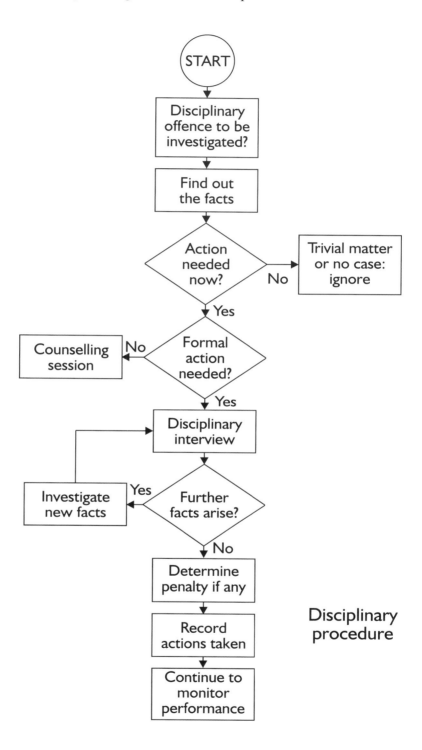

Disciplinary procedure

Activity 19

20 mins

This Activity may provide the basis of appropriate evidence for your S/NVQ portfolio. If you are intending to take this course of action, it might be better to write your answers on separate sheets of paper.

1   Explain how well you ensure that your team members are kept informed of the organization's disciplinary procedures.

_____

_____

_____

2   What actions do you intend to take to make them better informed? (Learn more yourself? Hold a team meeting? Talk to individuals? Or what other actions?)

_____

_____

_____

3   How confident are you that the contributions you make to implementing disciplinary and grievance procedures are consistent with your organization's values and policies?

_____

_____

_____

4   If you are less than totally confident about this, what actions will you take? (Talk to your manager? Talk to the Human Resources department? Some other action?)

_____

_____

_____

Record below the result of the actions taken in 2 and 4 above.

_____

_____

_____

_____

_____

5 Following the procedures

As all organizations have to cope with disciplinary problems, most of them have developed systematic procedures for handling them.

A **disciplinary procedure** is a set of written guidelines to help everyone at work – managers, team leaders, other employees and shop stewards, to deal with disciplinary matters.

Activity 20

3 mins

Why do you think a set of written guidelines is so important when dealing with discipline?

_____

_____

_____

_____

Previous legal cases have established that having unfair procedures, or not following procedures, will make a dismissal unfair, even if there is a good reason to discipline or dismiss someone.

To deal with discipline in a fair way, consistency is vital: everyone must be given the same treatment for the same offence. This makes it important that all team leaders and managers who deal with discipline do so in the same way. Without written guidelines, no one is quite sure how to act in a particular set of circumstances.

It makes sense to follow your organization's procedures when you have to deal with discipline.

The following extracts from an example of a good disciplinary procedure is taken with permission from _Discipline at Work – The ACAS Advisory Handbook_.

5.1 Sound procedures

(1) Purpose and scope

This procedure is designed to help and encourage all employees to achieve and maintain standards of conduct, attendance and job performance. The company rules (a copy of which is displayed in the office) and this procedure apply to all employees. The aim is to ensure consistent and fair treatment for all.

Notice that the procedure starts by stating:

- **what** the procedure is for;
- **where** the procedure can be seen;
- **to whom** it applies.

EXTENSION 2
Most organizations in this country base their disciplinary procedures on the ACAS Code of Practice No. 1: *Disciplinary practice and procedures in employment.* This code of practice is reproduced at the back of this workbook.

(2) Principles

a) No disciplinary action will be taken against an employee until the case has been fully investigated.

b) At every stage in the procedure the employee will be advised of the nature of the complaint against him or her and will be given the opportunity to state his or her case before any decision is made.

c) At all stages the employee will have the right to be accompanied by a shop steward, employee representative or work colleague during the disciplinary interview.

Activity 21

3 mins

Why is it good practice to allow someone who is under investigation to be represented by a union official or a colleague?

_____

_____

_____

_____

As you may have answered, having a union official or a friend of the alleged offender present can help to ensure there is 'fair play', and that the case is fully understood by the individual.

To continue with the ACAS example procedure:

d) No employee will be dismissed for the first breach of discipline except in the case of gross misconduct when the penalty will be dismissal without notice or payment in lieu of notice.

(We'll discuss what is meant by 'gross misconduct' shortly.)

e) An employee will have the right to appeal against any disciplinary penalty imposed.

f) The procedure may be implemented at any stage if the employee's alleged misconduct warrants such action.

Activity 22

Point (e) above is another 'essential ingredient' of a good disciplinary procedure.

Can you think of **one** reason why it is so important to allow an appeal against a penalty?

_____

_____

You may agree that allowing the right of appeal:

■ helps to make sure that justice is done;
■ reduces the possibility that someone will be harshly punished due to personal bias or animosity;
■ in the case of a dispute over the decision, allows fresh minds to be brought in.

Now we come to the main part of the procedure. Read the following extract carefully and note:

■ that there are a number of stages. (As was stated in the principles above, the procedure may be entered at any stage – it doesn't have to be followed step by step.)
■ each stage is a more serious step than the one before.

(3) The Procedure

Minor faults will be dealt with informally but where the matter is more serious the following procedure will be used:

Stage 1 – Oral warning

If conduct or performance does not meet acceptable standards the employee will normally be given a formal **oral warning**. He or she will be advised of the reason for the warning, that it is the first stage of the disciplinary procedure and of his or her right of appeal. A brief note of the oral warning will be kept but will be spent after . . . months, subject to satisfactory conduct and performance.

Stage 2 – Written warning

If the offence is a serious one, or if a further offence occurs, a **written warning** will be given to the employee by the first line manager. This will give details of the complaint, the improvement required and the timescale. It will warn that action under Stage 3 will be considered if there is no satisfactory improvement and will advise of the right of appeal. A copy of this written warning will be kept by the first line manager but it will be disregarded for disciplinary purposes after . . . months subject to satisfactory conduct and performance.

Stage 3 – Final written warning or disciplinary suspension

If there is still a failure to improve and conduct or performance is still unsatisfactory, or if the misconduct is sufficiently serious to warrant only one written warning but insufficiently serious to justify dismissal (in effect both first and final written warning), a **final written warning** will normally be given to the employee. This will give details of the complaint, will warn that dismissal will result if there is no satisfactory improvement and will advise of the right of appeal. A copy of this final written warning will be kept by the first line manager but it will be spent after … months (in exceptional cases the period may be longer) subject to satisfactory conduct and performance.

Alternatively, consideration will be given to imposing a penalty of a disciplinary suspension without pay for up to a maximum of five working days.

Stage 4 – Dismissal

If conduct or performance is still unsatisfactory and the employee still fails to reach the prescribed standards, **dismissal** will normally result. Only the appropriate senior manager can take the decision to dismiss. The employee will be provided, as soon as reasonably practicable, with written reasons for dismissal, the date on which employment will terminate and the right of appeal.

Activity 23

Answer the following questions about the procedure above by circling the appropriate box.

1   Would every minor offence have to be taken through the procedure above?

| YES | NO |

2   In which stages do the warnings given become spent or disregarded after a period of time?

| 1 | 2 | 3 | 4 |

3   After which stages does the employee have a right of appeal?

| 1 | 2 | 3 | 4 |

4   At which stages are the warnings written down?

| 1 | 2 | 3 | 4 |

5   At which stages does the employee receive a written document?

| 1 | 2 | 3 | 4 |

The answers to this activity can be found on page 83–4.

Now let's deal with what is meant by 'gross misconduct'.

Activity 24

Stealing would be classified as 'gross misconduct'. List **four** other disciplinary offences which you would expect to come into this category.

_____

_____

_____

_____

Let's see what ACAS suggest as examples of offences normally regarded as gross misconduct:

- theft, fraud or deliberate falsification of records;
- fighting, or assault on another person;
- deliberate damage to company property;
- serious incapability through alcohol or being under the influence of illegal drugs;
- serious negligence which causes unacceptable loss, damage or injury;
- serious acts of insubordination.

There isn't always universal agreement about what constitutes gross misconduct, and your organization may have different ideas.

One survey of British companies and local authorities found that gambling was considered by different organizations to be:

- a minor disciplinary offence;
- a major disciplinary offence;
- gross misconduct.

The procedure which we have discussed is just one example of a disciplinary procedure which could be used by an organization, and is intended as a model for a company writing its own procedure.

> **Your own organization will probably have its own procedure. That's the one you have to follow.**

6 Finding out the facts

The start of our disciplinary procedure diagram shows the first step to be taken:

Read the following case and then think about what further information you would need.

Activity 25

■ Mrs Jones, who works in the offices at her company, one day spends some time going round the other staff collecting money for a local hospital.

Those are all the facts as you know them. You are asked to decide whether Mrs Jones has committed a disciplinary offence by doing this.

What other information would you need to know, before making your judgement?

Jot down **four** questions you would ask.

_____

_____

_____

_____

Your questions may be included here.

■ How long did Mrs Jones take to make her collection?
■ What prompted her to do it?
■ Has she or anyone else in the organization done this sort of thing before?
■ Is there a well-known management rule about what she did?

- Is Mrs Jones's general record a good one?
- Is it important that she did not leave her desk?
- Did she get permission to make the collection?

When we find out the answers to these kind of questions, it becomes possible to decide about the case.

Here are two possible sets of circumstances.

Activity 26

6 mins

■ Mrs Jones works in the wages department. On Monday morning, she cleared up her work, and then went round her colleagues in the department to collect money for the purchase of equipment at a local hospital. She made this collection during an extended coffee break, taking about 45 minutes in all. The first person Mrs Jones collected from was her office first line manager. Everybody in the office knew that Mrs Jones's husband had been treated for cancer at the local hospital. It was also true that other people had collected for charities in the past.

Is this a disciplinary offence?
   YES   NO

What (briefly) are the reasons for your decision?

_____

_____

_____

■ Mrs Jones works as a receptionist at a local company. One Wednesday morning she repeatedly left the reception area unattended while visiting other offices to collect money. One way and another, the collection had taken most of the morning. Mrs Jones had tried to keep well clear of the office manager. She was collecting for the sports and social fund at the hospital where her husband works. She also collects every week for the football pools, and management had already warned her about the time she was taking on this.

Is this a disciplinary offence?
   YES   NO

What (briefly) are the reasons for your decision?

_____

_____

_____

Compare your answers with the response given on page 84.

The discussion following this Activity leads to the conclusion that:

it is important to make sure that as much relevant information as possible is collected about each case.

It is also important that this is done promptly, before memories of the incident fade.

One formula which can help us collect information thoroughly is the '5W' formula.

6.1 The 5W formula

This formula consists of five questions:

WHO?	WHEN?	WHAT?	WHERE?	WHY?

Let's look at them one at a time.

■ **Who?**

Disciplinary offences always involve people so we need to ask:

- **Who** was involved?
- **Who** were the witnesses?
- **Who** are the first line managers involved?
- **Who** is the trade union representative?

■ **When?**

It is always important to know when an incident happened. A whole argument can be destroyed if the wrong time or day is written down. For example, if the incident is mistakenly thought to have taken place on a Wednesday afternoon, and then the person under investigation is subsequently able to prove he or she was somewhere else at the time, the whole case collapses.

It is especially important to know whether the incident happened inside or outside working hours.

■ **What?**

Before any action can be contemplated, it is obviously vital to know exactly what happened. This is seldom as easy as it sounds. In many disciplinary cases there are likely to be different versions of the same event, especially where the misconduct is serious enough for dismissal. This is where your judgement comes in.

■ **Where?**

Establishing where a disciplinary offence took place is important for the record. For instance, smoking may be allowed in the canteen, but not on the petrol station forecourt. And if one of your team commits an offence in another section, another first line manager may have to be involved in the investigation.

■ **Why?**

The final question is to ask why the incident took place. The answer to this can make the difference between whether it is treated as a disciplinary case or not.

In asking **why**, we should remember two things:

- ■ why did the incident happen at that time or place?
- ■ why did it involve that particular person?

Activity 27

4 mins

■ The Cartwheel Company is a medium-sized firm operating three shifts. The shop floor is divided into a number of different sections, and normally two first line managers are on the night shift.

For two weeks now, one first line manager has been off sick and no proper cover has been arranged. Towards the end of the night shift, Harry Davies, one of the shop floor engineers, goes to see the only first line manager available. He complains that some of the men in his unit have set up a card school, and that they are never back from breaks on time. Harry claims to represent at least four other men in the section who are all fed up with carrying the extra work created by the others never being there on time.

Use the **who**, **when**, **what**, **where** and **why** formula to investigate this matter.

Write down the questions you would want answers to, in the space below.

Who? _____

_____

When? _____

_____

What? _____

_____

Where? _____

_____

Why? _____

_____

37

The following are typical questions drawn out by the 5W formula:

Who?

- **Who** were the members of the alleged card school?
- **Who** were those Harry said he represents?
- **Who** were the witnesses?
- **Who** were the first line managers?
- **Who** is the trade union representative?

When?

- **When** did the alleged card school sessions take place – dates and times?
- **When** did they start and finish – dates and times?

What?

- **What** did the card school involve? (Gambling for money, or was it just for fun?)
- **What** extra work did Harry and his colleagues have to do?
- **What** is the past record of this kind of offence?

Where?

- **Where** did the card school take place? (In the canteen? On the shop floor?)

Why?

- **Why** has Harry come to you? (Has he a personal grudge which has led him to blow up a small incident out of all proportion?)
- **Why** are the card games taking place? (Is the work badly organized?)
- **Why** has the information come to you in this way? (Does supervision need to be improved?)

I hope you agree with me that the 5W formula has succeeded in raising most of the important questions about the case.

Nevertheless, when you are investigating an incident like this, you will need continually to ask yourself:

is there anything more I need to know?

7 The counselling session

Let's remind ourselves of the first part of our procedure diagram for dealing with an alleged disciplinary offence:

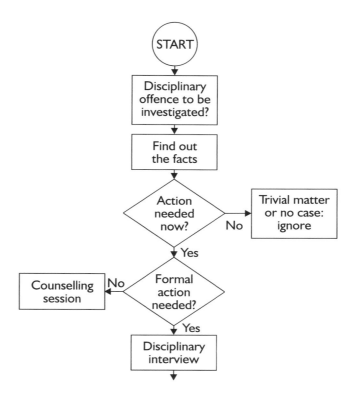

Once we have found out the facts of the case, we should know whether a disciplinary offence has been committed.

The question then arises:

Is action needed at this time?

If our judgement is that action is needed, there is another decision to be made:

Is it more appropriate to 'have a quiet word' with the offender, or is the offence serious enough to warrant a disciplinary interview?

In the next section, we'll look into the disciplinary interview. For the moment, let's examine what's involved in a counselling session or informal discussion.

Obviously, as a team leader, you are concerned to get a good performance from each member of your team which means that breaches of discipline cannot be tolerated for long. However, you have an important role in supporting your team members. An informal discussion is an opportunity to offer your support if it is needed. If a person is under-performing, it could be due to stress and personal difficulties. A friendly approach from you can mean a lot to a harassed employee.

■ Geoff Parks had been a first line manager for three years and his workteam hadn't changed much during that time.

One morning, Geoff saw Jed Tarrow, one of his team, walking across the yard. He noticed Jed wasn't wearing a safety helmet.

The next time Geoff saw Jed, they were both queuing at the staff canteen for lunch. They exchanged greetings and talked a while about a job Jed was working on. Then Geoff said:

'I noticed you in the yard yesterday without a helmet, Jed. That's very unlike you.'

'Sorry about that, boss. I was thinking about something else – don't know what made me forget.'

'You won't let it happen again, will you Jed? I look to you to set an example.'

You may deal with some minor breaches of discipline in a similar way yourself. Geoff knew that it would be enough to give Jed a gentle reminder. To have mentioned disciplinary procedures would not have helped here.

Compare this with the next case.

■ Lila Podesta was a bright but unpredictable young woman. She worked in a large dress shop and, because she had a flair for it, the manager, Hilda Grace, allowed her to do most of the window dressing. Lila knew she was good at this and had jokingly threatened to take her talents elsewhere if Hilda criticized her work in any way.

However, Lila 'took advantage' of her situation by repeatedly arriving to work late. Finally Hilda knew she'd have to do something. When Lila arrived one morning, half an hour late, she invited her into the office. This is what she said:

'Lila, I have a problem. Several of the other girls have complained to me that you are late to work every day, and I do nothing about it. What do you think I should do?'

'Tell me off, I suppose.'

'Lila, you are good at your job, but I think you are letting yourself down. I don't want to lose you, but wherever you work people won't put up with persistent lateness. Is there a particular problem at home?'

'Not really.'

'Well, we all have a job to do. I know that the company management won't allow me to take no action for very long. I have to ask you, to be fair to everyone else working here, to make an effort and get to work on time.'

Hilda knew that this was all she could do before invoking formal disciplinary procedures. She also knew that, if she did that, Lila would probably leave. It's the kind of difficult situation which you might have to deal with from time to time.

The rules are made for everyone. If someone breaks them, then sooner or later you have to take action.

Respect and confidentiality

One important aspect of dealing with disciplinary matters is that everyone deserves to be treated with respect, whether or not you believe them to have broken the rules.

Furthermore, all conversations between you and an individual regarding that person's conduct should be kept confidential. You may have to pass on information to those with a need to know it – your manager, perhaps, or the Human Resources department – but a breach of discipline is not something that should normally be discussed with other team members.

In many work situations, confidentiality can be difficult to maintain. When a group of people work closely together, for example, any unusual event may lead to speculation and gossip. The team leader plays a key role here, in:

- making it clear that information and views given in confidence are not for general consumption;

- setting an example by not joining in gossip about team members or other colleagues;

- not, under normal circumstances, discussing the behaviour of one team member with another;

- if possible, putting a halt to gossip by providing clear-cut information, but without disclosing anything that is not the concern of those not directly involved.

Fine lines must sometimes be trod. It is worth remembering that what counts above everything is the way the team leader behaves. If he or she can earn the respect of the team, and they know that their leader is incorruptible and trustworthy in all things, problems of this kind will tend not to arise.

Activity 28

15 mins

This Activity may provide the basis of appropriate evidence for your S/NVQ portfolio. If you are intending to take this course of action, it might be better to write your answers on separate sheets of paper.

Two sets of self-searching questions for you.

1   When dealing with matters of discipline, are you scrupulous in treating individuals with respect, whatever their suspected misdemeanour?

_____

Do you feel that others in your organization always maintain respect for the individual, during disciplinary interviews and the like?

_____

Explain in what way, if at all, you intend to modify your approach, in this regard. If you need evidence for your S/NVQ portfolio, you should:

■ describe one or more particular incidents in the past in some detail (omitting the names of individuals if you wish), which you thought were not handled well;

■ explain in detail how you will modify your disciplinary procedures, so that anyone accused of a disciplinary offence is treated with proper respect;

■ explain how you intend to ensure that your modified procedures will be followed. (For example, you may decide to discuss your proposals with someone from the Human Resources department, and invite them to monitor your disciplinary interviews.)

_____

_____

_____

_____

2   Does gossip tend to be rife among your team members, especially when something occurs that requires disciplinary action to be taken?

_____

_____

Explain how you usually deal with this kind of problem.

_____

_____

Now explain what you think you might do differently in this regard, in the future. Again, for portfolio evidence, you must be very specific about the changes you will make, and your proposed method for ensuring these changes are followed.

_____

_____

_____

_____

_____

_____

8 Taking action

Once it is decided that formal action is to be taken, a disciplinary interview must take place.

From our procedure diagram we can see the stages to be followed:

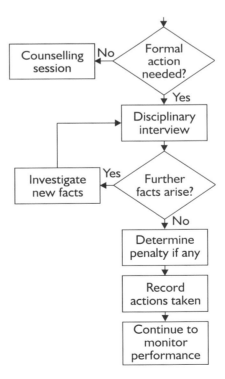

8.1 The purpose of an interview

The purposes of a disciplinary interview are to:

- allow the employee to give his or her version of the incident;
- ensure a full discussion, so that everyone present has a chance to hear the facts and to present any new facts;
- advise the employee of his or her rights;
- enable a fair judgement to be made so that an appropriate penalty can be imposed.

Before the interview, we have to **prepare**.

8.2 Preparing for the interview

Let's remind ourselves of the case we looked at earlier.

- The Cartwheel Company is a medium-sized firm operating three shifts. The shop floor is divided into a number of different sections, and normally two first line managers are on the night shift.

  For two weeks now, one first line manager has been off sick and no proper cover has been arranged. Towards the end of the night shift, Harry Davies, one of the shop floor engineers, goes to see the only first line manager available. He complains that some of the men in his unit have set up a card school, and that they are never back from breaks on time. Harry claims to represent at least four other men in the section who are all fed up with carrying the extra work created by the others never being there on time.

In order to prepare for the interview, we can apply our '5W' formula once more.

Activity 29

6 mins

Use the 5W formula by answering each of the following questions. You only need give **one** answer to each question.

What is the meeting about?

_____

_____

Why do we need this meeting?

_____

_____

Who should be at the meeting?

_____

_____

Where should the meeting take place?

_____

_____

When should the meeting take place?

_____

_____

Compare your answers with the following.

■ **What** is the meeting about?

It is alleged that a card school has been started.

■ **Why** do we need this meeting?

Because this could well be a disciplinary offence.

■ **Who** should be at the meeting?

- Witnesses – to confirm the truth of the report.
- Other first line managers – to find out what they know or may have already done.
- The union representative – to keep them in the picture, and to represent the people being accused.
- The person or persons accused of the offence.

■ **Where** should the meeting take place?

Some quiet area away from the workplace is much more likely to result in a satisfactory interview than in a noisy area, or where others might overhear.

■ **When** should the meeting take place?

We need to give ourselves time to prepare for the interview, so we shouldn't rush into it. We may also need to check on when the participants are available, and what times might cause the minimum disruption of work.

8.3 The interview

Something which nobody looks forward to – which is all the more reason for handling it absolutely by the book.

Activity 30

3 mins

How should an interview begin?

_____

_____

_____

_____

Like any other kind of meeting, an interview should start by introducing the people present and saying what the purpose of the meeting is.

■ Let's imagine the person alleged to be the leading member of the card school is called Ray Cooley. Ray has been asked to attend the interview so that we can hear what he's got to say, and eventually to determine what further action should be taken.

Compare the two ways of starting the interview:

1 The first line manager meets Ray on the shop floor.

'Look here, Ray, I know you're running a card school, so don't deny it. Nobody's getting any work done in your section and I'm sick to the back teeth with complaints. I'm giving you a written warning. Now get back to work.'

2 The first line manager arranges the interview in an office. The shop steward is present.

'Sit yourself down, Ray. You've been asked to come along today because it has been reported that you have been running a card school during the firm's time. I've checked it out and it seems you are involved, so I've called you in to have a chat about it. I think you know the other people here. You know that playing cards during working hours is against company rules, so let's hear what you've got to say.'

> However angry you may feel, it's important not to lose your temper. If you do, your behaviour could be considered in law as unreasonable.

The first approach is likely to put Ray's back up and lead to conflict.

The second approach is much more likely to be profitable. It encourages Ray to talk and shows that no one has prejudged the case.

A courteous but firm manner is needed. It is important to encourage the employee to talk about the offence.

During the interview, it is best not to make any decisions straight away, especially where the case is a serious one.

Give yourself time to think. Adjourn the interview before you come to a conclusion.

And, most importantly:

keep a cool head – don't get emotionally involved.

8.4 The decision

Eventually a decision must be made.

Activity 31

2 mins

What procedure should be used to decide the further action to be taken?

_____

Look on page 84 for feedback to this Activity.

This is how one first line manager ended his interview with our alleged card player, Ray Cooley.

Activity 32

4 mins

■ 'Right, Ray, this is the last time I want to see you in here. I'll get to the bottom of this card school affair and you'll end up being disciplined. I'm warning you not to get involved again. That's my decision, and it's final, so get out of my office.'

_____

Bearing in mind what the first line manager is supposed to be doing here, how many things can you find wrong with the statement above?

_____

_____

_____

You may have noticed a number of problems with this first line manager's approach. Perhaps they are included here.

- It is not clear what decision – if any – has been made.
- It is not clear what sort of warning Ray has been given.
- The first line manager hasn't asked the union (or other) representative to comment.
- It is not clear what the first line manager is going to do next.
- Ray hasn't been told of his right to appeal.
- Ray hasn't been asked to respond to the statement.

I hope you agree that there are better ways to end interviews.

Activity 33

5 mins

Read through this account of another first line manager talking to Ray Cooley, and note down the good points.

- First line manager: Right, Ray, let's just sum up then. You admit that on three separate occasions – we've got the dates here – you were involved in a card school during working time. You also know that was against the work rules. Do you agree?

  Ray: Yes.

  Shop steward: Agreed.

  First line manager: You understand that under the agreed procedure, I can give you a verbal warning for a first offence, and that is what I intend to do. Do you accept that, Ray?

  Ray: Fair enough.

  Shop steward: That seems fair if it's consistent with what happened to the others.

  First line manager: Yes, you've been involved in all the cases, so we know we are being consistent.

  OK, Ray, so this is an official verbal warning which will be confirmed to me by your union and the Human Resources department. This is the first stage of the company's disciplinary procedure. It will stay on record for six months – that will take us to the 15th of August – and if there are no more problems we will wipe the slate clean then.

  If you do offend again, you should be aware that this will lead to further stages of the disciplinary procedure, and may eventually result in your being dismissed. You do have a right of appeal against this penalty, and if you want to do so, you should let Mr Renwick know by Friday.

  Any final questions?

Note down the good points.

_____

_____

_____

_____

_____

Look on page 85 for feedback on this activity.

8.5 After the interview

It may be tempting to heave a sigh of relief and put the matter behind you but it is very important to complete the process thoroughly.

Activity 34

What more is there to be done, following the disciplinary interview?

_____

_____

_____

If you recall the last part of our procedure diagram:

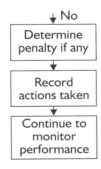

you can see that there are two more main actions:

■ **to write down the actions which have been taken**

It is the job of the person holding the interview to record what took place. In some workplaces, the Human Resources department may take on this task.

■ **to continue to monitor the behaviour of the person penalized for the offence**

If the employee is in your team, it will be your job to keep an eye on the team member.

49

Let's summarize the main points to remember.

- **Prepare** by:

  - making sure you have all the information you will need;
  - letting everyone involved know when and where the interview is to be held;
  - giving the employee time to prepare.

- **At the interview:**

  - introduce everyone present, explaining why they are there;
  - allow the employee to state his or her case;
  - keep the tone of the interview formal but courteous – don't lose your temper;
  - consider adjourning the interview to give time for a considered decision;
  - explain clearly what decision has been made and what further action is to be taken.

- **After the interview:**

  - record the action taken;
  - continue to monitor the situation.

Records must be complete and accurate. According to ACAS, records should include:

- details of the nature of any breach of disciplinary rules;
- the action taken and the reasons for it;
- whether an appeal was lodged;
- its outcome and any subsequent developments.

These records should be carefully safeguarded and kept confidential.

Except in agreed special circumstances breaches of disciplinary rules should be disregarded after a specified period of satisfactory conduct.

Remember that if you keep records about individuals on computer, you may be subject to the Data Protection Act 1984. This obliges data users to register with the Data Protection Registrar if the data they keep falls within the Act, and failure to do this can lead to a large fine. The intent of the Act is to protect information about individuals, and to set up a mechanism whereby people can have access to information held about them.

Activity 35

15 mins

This Activity may provide the basis of appropriate evidence for your S/NVQ portfolio. If you are intending to take this course of action, it might be better to write your answers on separate sheets of paper.

Are the records you keep concerning disciplinary matters always complete and accurate?   YES   NO

Do they always include details of the nature of any breach of disciplinary rules?   YES   NO

Do they always record the action taken and the reasons for it?   YES   NO

Do they always indicate whether an appeal was lodged?   YES   NO

Do they always note the outcome and subsequent developments?   YES   NO

Are the records always carefully safeguarded and kept confidential?   YES   NO

If you answered NO to any of the questions above, explain in what way your records are deficient, or have been in the past. (For S/NVQ portfolio evidence, you should produce copies of your records if possible.)

_____

_____

_____

_____

Does your organization satisfy the requirements of the Data Protection Act 1984?   YES   NO   Don't know

Now write down any actions you plan to take as a result of your answers to these questions, to ensure that your disciplinary records conform both to the ACAS recommendations, and to your organization's legal requirements. For S/NVQ portfolio evidence, you should write out very specific plans, and show how these will help your records conform. At the first opportunity, a copy of your new improved records should be included.

_____

_____

_____

_____

Of course, it may not be your job to keep disciplinary records, or to ensure conformity with the law. But if your team members are involved, you will no doubt want to know that proper records are being kept, and you may be expected to input information into those records.

Self-assessment 3

1 Name one thing that all disciplinary offences involve.

_____

2 If a disciplinary offence is minor, a first line manager might decide that beginning the formal disciplinary procedure is unnecessary. What else might they do in this case?

_____

_____

3 Who benefits from there being clear rules for dealing with disciplinary offences?

_____

_____

4 Imagine that you have investigated a case and decided that formal action needs to be taken. Now you have to prepare for and hold a disciplinary interview.

Here is a list of possible actions you might take. Pick out **seven** actions from the list and place them in the correct order, so as to describe an appropriate sequence of actions to be taken.

a Decide what penalty should be imposed.
b Decide where the meeting is to be held.
c Hold a counselling session.
d Continue to monitor performance.
e Decide who should be present.
f Introduce the participants, and state why they are there.
g Decide whether the case is serious enough for formal action.
h Sum up what's been said.
i Give the employee a chance to state his or her case.

_____

_____

Answers to these questions can be found on page 83.

9 Summary

- The actions involved in dealing with a disciplinary offence are:

  - find out the **facts**;
  - decide whether action is needed;
  - decide between formal action and informal action.

- If formal action is needed:

  - hold a disciplinary interview;
  - if further facts arise, investigate them;
  - determine penalty to be imposed, if any;
  - record the actions taken;
  - continue to monitor performance.

- An offence involves a breach of the rules.

- Every well-run sizeable organization should have a written disciplinary procedure.

- First line managers should always follow procedures when dealing with discipline.

- Records about disciplinary matters must be complete and accurate. They should include: details of breach of disciplinary rules; the action taken and the reasons for it; whether an appeal was lodged; its outcome and any subsequent developments.

  These records should be carefully safeguarded and kept confidential, and may be subject to the requirements of the Data Protection Act 1984.

Session D Dismissal

1 Introduction

No one ever said that being a first line manager was easy! Occasionally, when employees do not respond positively to disciplinary procedures, so that their performance or behaviour does not improve, the stage may be reached when they have to be dismissed. It could be that you have already had to dismiss someone in your own team.

Dismissal may seem harsh on the employee, but it is done for the good of the rest of the workforce. Persistent poor performance or bad behaviour can have a very disruptive and demotivating effect on other workers. It is frequently the case that, once an individual has been dismissed, the atmosphere in the workteam lightens considerably, and efficiency goes up.

Of course, when you are considering something as serious as dismissal, it is vital that established procedures are followed to the letter.

Let's begin by looking at the ways in which dismissal can come about.

2 The meaning of dismissal

Dismissal occurs when:

- The employer terminates the employment.
- The employee resigns because the employer has broken the contract and/or has acted in a very unreasonable manner by treating the employee unfairly in some way or other. Some examples are:

  - not following disciplinary procedures;
  - directing personal abuse towards or swearing at an employee.

  This is known as **constructive dismissal**.

- A fixed-term contract runs out and isn't renewed.
- An employer refuses to let a woman return to work after the birth of her baby, even though she has a legal right to do so.

Dismissal can be fair or unfair.

As was mentioned earlier:

not following the procedures may make a dismissal unfair, even if there are good grounds for dismissal.

55

3 Grounds for dismissal

There are five grounds for dismissing someone fairly:

> Whatever the grounds for dismissal, the law requires the employer to act **fairly** in relying on that reason for dismissal.

1 because of the employee's **misconduct**;

2 because of the employee's lack of **capability** or **qualification**;

3 **redundancy**;

4 a reason related to **the law**;

5 some **other substantial reason**.

Activity 36

3 mins

Read these two short cases.

- Will Greenwood was seen removing a fuse from a plug, which stopped a machine working. He said he wanted to give everyone a break! Will already had a poor work record, and he was later dismissed.

- Janet Hannah never seemed to be at work on a Friday. She had been warned in accordance with the company's disciplinary procedure and was eventually dismissed.

Tick the general reason for dismissal that applies to both these cases:

Misconduct ☐

Redundancy ☐

Related to the law ☐

Lack of capability or qualification ☐

Some other substantial reason ☐

In both cases, it was the conduct or behaviour of the person that led to their dismissal. Their actions brought them into conflict with company rules. So **misconduct** is the correct response here.

Activity 37

Look at this case.

- Alan Milburn is a french polisher, but his trade is gradually disappearing in his company as wood is replaced by laminates. His employer eventually has to tell Alan that there is no more work for him, so he will have to leave.

Tick the general reason for dismissal.

Misconduct	☐
Redundancy	☐
Related to the law	☐
Lack of capability or qualification	☐
Some other substantial reason	☐

The reason for Alan being asked to leave is lack of work. In other words, his job is not needed. This is known as **redundancy**.

Redundancy occurs when an organization has to reduce its staff levels. It might be a particular job which is no longer needed, as in the case above, or it may be caused by a general downturn in business, so that many employees become redundant.

Redundancy can result in:

- compulsory dismissals;
- voluntary resignations;
- natural wastage;
- employee transfers to other jobs.

When making someone redundant, an employer is obliged to pay the employee:

- any wages owed;
- any holiday pay owed;
- pay in lieu of notice if the employee has not been given the proper period of notice;
- redundancy payment, if the employee qualifies.

The employee is normally entitled to a redundancy payment from the employer if he or she has:

- been employed continuously by that employer for at least two years, and
- is aged between twenty and sixty-four years.

The amount is based on the number of years worked, and the weekly pay. The weekly pay taken into account is subject to a maximum amount, set by the Government and reviewed each year.

Activity 38

3 mins

Now read these two short cases.

- An engineering company takes on Stewart Turner as a lathe operator. After three months' trial period, it is clear that Stewart hasn't the ability to get on with the work, so he is dismissed.

- James Pickering is taken on as a nurse in a children's playgroup. It is later discovered that he has no qualifications for the job and that the children are suffering as a result.
  Note down the general reason for dismissal that would apply to both cases.

Misconduct	☐
Redundancy	☐
Related to the law	☐
Lack of capability or qualification	☐
Some other substantial reason	☐

In both these cases, it was the **capability,** or **qualification** to do the job, that was called into question. If someone cannot do a job satisfactorily, then it is fair to dismiss them, provided care was taken in appointing them and in giving reasonable training.

Activity 39

3 mins

If you find that a member of your workteam is not doing a job as well as you would like, what action should you take?

Dismiss the person on the grounds of lack of capability?	☐
Give the person extra training and coaching?	☐
Try to find out if there is any special reason for the unsatisfactory work?	☐

You may well do all of these – but not in the order given! Before contemplating dismissing anyone for lack of capability, they should be given every chance to improve. This may mean investigating to see if there is any particular reason for poor work, and/or providing extra training and coaching.

Activity 40

3 mins

Here are two more short cases for you to consider:

■ John Newton worked as a travelling salesman. Then he committed a driving offence and his driving licence was taken away. The only practical way that John could manage to visit all his customers was by car, so he was dismissed.

■ Mr Bagley had employed Gretta to work behind the counter in his shop. He then found out that Gretta was still of school age and so he dismissed her.

Note down the general reason for dismissal that would seem to apply to these two cases.

Misconduct ☐

Redundancy ☐

Related to the law ☐

Lack of capability or qualification ☐

Some other substantial reason ☐

You may have answered that John was no longer qualified to do his job; this is true. Another way of looking at it is to say that to continue to employ him doing the same job would be to break the law.

In Gretta's case, it would have been illegal for Mr Bagley to continue to employ her, as she was under age. In other words, the reasons were to do with the **law**.

The four categories we've covered so far are the most common valid reasons for dismissing someone. However, other situations can arise which result in dismissal. The category 'some other substantial reason' is a kind of catch-all which covers all cases not included in the main four reasons we've discussed.

The key word here is substantial. The employer must, if necessary, be able to persuade an Industrial Tribunal that the reason for dismissal was substantial. This fifth category is not meant to be an easy way to justify getting rid of unwanted employees.

Now let's look at unfair dismissal.

4 Unfair dismissal

In this section we'll take a look at some aspects of unfair dismissal.

4.1 People who can complain

To be able to claim that you were unfairly dismissed, you must be an employee – and not a contractor for example.

You must also have completed two years' continuous employment with your employer. Since the enactment of the Employment Protection (Part-Time Employees) Regulations 1995, this qualifying period applies to both full- and part-time employees, regardless of how many hours they work each week.

Employees who are over retirement age for a certain job can't normally complain about unfair dismissal. For instance, Fire Service employees retire earlier than people in other occupations; if they are kept on it is usually by 'grace and favour'.

4.2 Constructive dismissal

If the employer breaks the contract of employment – say by demoting an employee to a lower position with lower pay – the employee may go to an Industrial Tribunal with a claim for constructive dismissal.

■ Joanna Smythe, a qualified accountant, who had worked in the accounts department of her organization for three years, was one morning told to carry out other duties in the general administrative section. Two weeks later, her salary was reduced. The company offered no good reason for this action, so Joanna resigned. She later claimed that she had been constructively dismissed, and she won her case.

It has to be said that these kind of claims do not always succeed. The Tribunal will ask whether 'the employer acted reasonably taking into account all the circumstances'. Sometimes an employer is compelled by circumstances to change the terms and conditions of employment. (It is not unknown for people to take a reduction in pay willingly, in order to help the company survive.)

60

4.3 Pregnancy and confinement

Provided she meets the qualifying conditions, an employee has the right to complain of unfair dismissal if her employer dismisses her because she is pregnant, unless:

EXTENSION 3
Further information on this subject is given in the DfEE booklet *Maternity Rights – A Guide for Employers and Employees.*

- her condition makes it impossible to do that job properly; or
- it would be against the law to do that job while pregnant.

For dismissal to be fair, the employer must either:

- have no suitable vacancy; or
- if there is a suitable vacancy, offer it to her.

What about the rights of a woman to come back to work after confinement?

Provided she meets certain qualifying conditions, an employee is entitled to return to her former job within a specified period after being away on maternity leave. If the job no longer exists because of redundancy, she is entitled to be offered a suitable alternative job if there is one available.

4.4 Other grounds

There are a number of other valid grounds for complaining of unfair dismissal, including:

- dismissal on grounds of sex or race discrimination;
- unfair selection on grounds of redundancy;
- dismissal related to trade union membership or activities.

5 Making a complaint

When an employee wants to complain about being dismissed unfairly, he or she may make an application to an **Industrial Tribunal**.

This must be done within three months of termination of employment.

An Industrial Tribunal is an independent body set up to hear cases of infringement of statutory employment rights. It is intended to provide a quick and inexpensive service, which is easily accessible by members of the public.

EXTENSION 4
The Department for Education and Employment booklet ITL 1 *Industrial Tribunal Procedure* gives further details.

Industrial tribunals have a chairman with legal experience, together with two lay assessors – one nominated by the Trades Union Congress (TUC) and the other by the Confederation of British Industry (CBI). The lay assessors are not there to take sides, but are chosen for their experience and practical knowledge of the work environment.

5.1 Going to a tribunal

EXTENSION 5
There are tribunal offices in the major British towns. Nearly all the hearings are open to the public, and it is worth going to see one, particularly if you are likely to be involved in a case.

Someone wishing to complain of unfair dismissal can get a copy of the application form from an Employment Service Jobcentre.

When a form is received by the Central Office of the Industrial Tribunals, copies are sent to the employer and to a conciliation officer at ACAS.

The conciliation officer will usually contact the parties involved and try to get them to reach a settlement rather than go to a hearing.

A tribunal rarely exceeds a day and, at the end of the hearing, a decision will be made. The 'remedies' for unfair dismissal are:

- reinstatement of the employee: giving the employee his or her old job back, without any loss of continuity of employment;
- re-engagement in a different position within the company;
- compensation.

Self-assessment 4

6 mins

1   Fill in the blanks in the following sentences with suitable words:

There are five grounds for dismissing someone fairly:

- because of the employee's _____;
- because of the employee's lack of _____ or _____;
- redundancy;
- a reason related to the _____;
- some other _____ reason.

2   A woman who has been on _____ _____ normally has the right to her old job back.

3   How can an employee claim unfair dismissal?

    _____

    _____

4   How long must someone have been employed before they can claim unfair dismissal?

    _____

5   If an employee wins a case against an employer for unfair dismissal, he or she may receive compensation, or else be reinstated or re-engaged. What's the difference between reinstatement and re-engagement?

_____

_____

_____

Answers to these questions can be found on page 83.

6 Summary

- There are five grounds for dismissing someone fairly:

    - because of the employee's **misconduct**;
    - because of the employee's lack of **capability** or **qualification**;
    - **redundancy**;
    - a reason related to **the law**;
    - some **other substantial reason**.

- Whatever the grounds for dismissal, the law requires the employer to act **fairly** in relying on that reason for dismissal.

- To be able to claim that you were unfairly dismissed, you must have completed two years' continuous employment with your employer.

- If the employer breaks the contract of employment, the employee may go to an Industrial Tribunal with a claim for constructive dismissal.

- When an employee wants to complain about being dismissed unfairly, he or she must make an application to an **Industrial Tribunal**.

Performance checks

Jot down the answers to the following questions on *Managing Lawfully –
People and Employment* .

Question 1   List **two** items that must be included in a written statement of the main
terms and conditions of employment.

_____

_____

Question 2   What is meant by 'implied terms' in a contract?

_____

_____

Question 3   Name **two** typical implied obligations on the part of the employee.

_____

_____

Question 4   What is meant by 'statutory terms' in a contract?

_____

_____

Question 5   Summarize, briefly, the **three** levels of organization of trade unions.

_____

_____

Question 6   It is said that a trade union shop steward has **three** separate roles. What is
meant by this?

_____

_____

Question 7   What is collective bargaining?

_____

_____

65

Question 8   There are four main objectives of discipline at work. Name **three** of them.

_____

_____

Question 9   Which **three** groups of employees need special care and attention by the first line manager, to ensure that they understand the organization's disciplinary rules.

_____

_____

Question 10   There are four suggested stages of a disciplinary procedure, each stage requiring a stronger action than the last. Name **three** of them.

_____

_____

Question 11   List **three** offences that would normally be considered as constituting 'gross misconduct'.

_____

_____

Question 12   We discussed four purposes of a disciplinary interview. List **three** of these.

_____

_____

Question 13   There are five grounds for dismissing someone fairly. Name **three** of them.

_____

_____

Question 14   How long must a temporary employee have worked before being able to claim unfair dismissal?

_____

_____

Question 15   How can an employee be 'constructively dismissed'?

Answers to these questions can be found on pages 85–6.

2 Workbook assessment

Read the following case incident, and then deal with the questions that follow. Write your answers on a separate sheet of paper.

■ Andrew Scarsbrook works in the drawing office at GHI Ltd. He has been employed for three years and has a reasonably good disciplinary record.

He usually arrives early for work – about half an hour before everybody else, and leaves half an hour early. This is no problem, as the company works a flexitime system which allows staff to clock in and out when they want to.

Doug Miller, the drawing office first line manager, has become suspicious of Andrew's work. Although he arrives half an hour early, Andrew does not often seem to do any extra work by the time the others arrive.

Doug thinks Andrew might be working on his own account. Doug does not tell anybody, but decides one morning to turn up early himself and see what Andrew is doing.

When he arrives, Doug goes straight to Andrew's desk and asks to look at the plans he is working on. Andrew pulls something out from under the pile, but Doug can see clearly that he is working on designs for a house extension. The company's work is solely in the commercial field, so Doug confronts Andrew.

Doug: Right, I can see you are doing your own work. I've been watching you for some time. You can pack up your things and I'll take you to see Mr Blakesly in Human Resources when he arrives.

Andrew: It's only a small piece of work, Mr Miller. It's only taken me ten minutes and I haven't done it before. It won't happen again. There's no need to take this further.

Doug: I'm afraid there is. I've been watching you for some time. Doing private work in company time amounts to stealing, and that's gross misconduct. As far as I'm concerned, you are for the sack.

Later in the morning, Andrew is called in to see the Human Resources Director David Blakesly. Mr Blakesly has already heard Doug's version of the events. He asks Andrew if he has anything to say. Andrew admits doing the private work that morning, but says again that it is the first time. In spite of this, Mr Blakesly confirms that doing private work in the firm's time is a serious disciplinary offence. He adds that he cannot afford to set a precedent by letting Andrew off the hook, so he is backing his first line manager and giving Andrew one week's notice. Andrew replies that he will be claiming unfair dismissal at an Industrial Tribunal.

The company's disciplinary procedure is based on the ACAS procedure we looked at in the workbook. Instant dismissal is appropriate in the case of gross misconduct, and stealing is included in this category.

The procedure has been agreed with the trade union. Andrew is a member of the union.

You only need write one or two sentences against each question.

1   What alternatives were open to Doug?

2   What alternatives were open to David Blakesly?

3   What points are likely to be taken into account by anyone (such as the ACAS conciliation officer, or the officers at the tribunal) when judging the fairness of the dismissal?

4   What do you think will be the outcome of the case, and why?

 Portfolio of evidence C15.2 | # 3 Work-based assignment

60 mins

The time guide for this assignment gives you an approximate idea of how long it is likely to take you to write up your findings. You will find you need to spend some additional time gathering information, talking to colleagues, and thinking about the assignment.

Your written response to this assignment may provide the basis of appropriate evidence for your S/NVQ portfolio. The assignment is also designed to help you to demonstrate the following Personal Competences:

■   thinking and taking decisions;
■   building teams;
■   focusing on results;
■   striving for excellence.

What you have to do

The purpose of this assignment is to allow you to apply recognized disciplinary procedures, and to follow the principles of good practice we have discussed.

If your organization has a written disciplinary procedure, get hold of a copy and read it through. If your organization does not have a written disciplinary procedure, use the ACAS example procedure we discussed in the workbook. (It is reproduced in Extension 2 on pages 75–81.)

You should ideally supervise, or at least support another manager in conducting, a disciplinary procedure, including an interview. Assuming you have an opportunity to do this in the near future, you should write a short report (around a page will do), describing:

■ what the alleged offence was;
■ the actions taken to investigate the incident;
■ the warning or other disciplinary measure meted out to the individual(s) concerned;
■ the proposed further action, should the offence be repeated.

Should you find that you have absolutely no opportunity to take part in a disciplinary procedure, you can, as a last resort, get together with one or more colleagues to simulate a disciplinary procedure through role play. Suitable imaginary situations might be:

1   You find one of your workteam in the rest room smoking when he or she should be working.

2   You find a group of your people waiting at the clocking out station ten minutes before leaving time, against company rules.

3   You learn that one of your workteam has stolen a colleague's leather jacket.

4   You notice a piece of valuable equipment is missing and later learn that one of the workteam has borrowed it for temporary use at home.

5   An employee is given a task, but fails to complete it properly. Later the partially completed work is found hidden away at the back of a cupboard. The employee has apparently placed it there hoping it won't be discovered.

One person should pretend to be accused of an offence. Others then proceed to investigate the alleged offence, to interview the accused, and to decide on a course of action. Again, you should write down what took place, in the form of a report.

Reflect and review

1 Reflect and review

Now that you have completed your work on *Managing Lawfully – People and Employment*, let us review each of our workbook objectives.

The first objective was:

■ When you have worked through this workbook you will be better able to explain what a contract of employment is, and what should be contained in a written statement of terms and conditions

Contracts of employment are very important, because they define the agreement between an employer and an employee. As we discussed, although a contract of employment doesn't have to be written down, employers are obliged to provide a written statement of the main terms and conditions. When changing a contract, both parties need to agree on the changes if difficulties are not to arise.

There are frequent changes to employment law, and as with all aspects of employment, it pays to keep up with the law.

■ Are you confident that all your team members' written statements of terms and conditions are legal and up to date? If not, what action should you take?

_____

_____

_____

■ Is your knowledge of employment law sufficient and up to date? If not, how can you learn more?

_____

_____

_____

The next objective was:

■ When you have worked through this workbook you will be better able to understand, and work effectively with, trade union representatives.

Trade unions exist to represent the interests of their members. They will support individuals or groups by negotiating with managers and providing members with expert advice and representation on disciplinary proceedings and to Industrial Tribunals. Shop stewards have a difficult job to do, and, by and large, will seek to co-operate in the best interests of employers and employees.

Although the powers of trade unions have declined in recent years, they are still key players in the work environment. It may be part of your job to work with their representatives, to help make your workplace safer and fairer.

■ How might you become better informed about the trade unions at your place of work?

_____

_____

_____

■ What other actions might you take to help make your dealings with unions more effective?

_____

_____

_____

The third objective was:

■ When you have worked through this workbook you will be better able to deal with disciplinary problems in a fair and consistent way.

Dealing with discipline is never easy and a systematic approach is needed in order to achieve fairness and consistency. Good management of discipline calls for written rules and procedures, based on the principles of justice and improving standards.

As we have seen, the overall procedure for dealing with discipline needs to start at investigating the facts and, when the appropriate action has been taken, continue by monitoring the behaviour of the offender. Using the diagram shown in the workbook you should be able to identify each step involved. By following your own organization's procedure (or alternatively the ACAS example procedure), you should now be very knowledgeable about what a good disciplinary procedure consists of.

■ If you have encountered difficulties when dealing with discipline, how might you get more help, either from within or outside your organization?

_____

_____

_____

■ How could you learn more about disciplinary procedures – perhaps by reading the ACAS handbook, or your own organization's procedures manual?

_____

_____

_____

The last objective was:

■ When you have worked through this workbook you will be better able to explain the law relating to dismissal.

The grounds on which someone may be fairly dismissed are very specific under the law. The procedures for appealing against unfair dismissal are also well defined. After reading this workbook, and if necessary referring to relevant DfEE and ACAS publications, you should be in a good position to explain the main points of the law related to dismissal.

■ Are you satisfied that you are well enough informed about dismissal? If not, what action will you take?

_____

_____

_____

2 Action plan

Use this plan to further develop for yourself a course of action you want to take. Make a note in the left-hand column of the issues or problems you want to tackle, and then decide what you intend to do, and make a note in Column 2.

The resources you need might include time, materials, information or money. You may need to negotiate for some of them, but they could be something easily acquired, like half an hour of somebody's time, or a chapter of a book. Put whatever you need in Column 3. No plan means anything without a timescale, so put a realistic target completion date in Column 4.

Finally, describe the outcome you want to achieve as a result of this plan, whether it is for your own benefit or advancement, or a more efficient way of doing things.

Desired outcomes

1 Issues

2 Action

3 Resources

4 Target completion

Actual outcomes

3 Extensions

Extension 1

Book   *The ACAS Employment Handbook*
Edition   1994
Publisher The Advisory, Conciliation and Arbitration Service (ACAS)

This and a number of other useful and inexpensive publications are available from ACAS Reader Ltd, P.O. Box 16, East Shilton, Leicester LE9 8ZZ. Tel: 01455 852225

Extension 2

Book   *Discipline at Work – The ACAS Advisory Handbook*
Edition   1996
Publisher The Advisory, Conciliation and Arbitration Service (ACAS)

Available from ACAS Reader Ltd, P.O. Box 16, East Shilton, Leicester LE9 8ZZ. Tel: 01455 852225

This book is based on the ACAS Code of Practice No. 1, the whole of which is reproduced below. (You are recommended to get hold of a copy of the book, as it contains much helpful advice, aside from the Code of Practice.)

ACAS Code of Practice No. 1

Introduction

1 **This document gives practical guidance on how to draw up disciplinary rules and procedures and how to operate them effectively. Its aim is to help employers and trade unions as well as individual employees – both men and women – wherever they are employed regardless of the size of the organization in which they work. In the smaller establishments it may not be practicable to adopt all the detailed provisions, but most of the features listed in paragraph 10 could be adopted and incorporated into a simple procedure.**

Why have disciplinary rules and procedures?

2 Disciplinary rules and procedures are necessary for promoting fairness and order in the treatment of individuals and in the conduct of industrial relations. They also assist an organization to operate effectively. Rules set standards of conduct at work; procedure helps to ensure that the standards are adhered to and also provides a fair method of dealing with alleged failures to observe them.

3 It is important that employees know what standards of conduct are expected of them and the Contracts of Employment Act 1972 (as amended by the Employment Protection Act 1975) requires employers to provide written

information for their employees about certain aspects of their disciplinary rules and procedures.*

*Section 1 of the Employment Protection (Consolidation) Act 1978 requires employers to provide employees with a written statement of the main terms and conditions of their employment. Section 13 of the Employment Act 1989 amends the Employment Protection (Consolidation) Act 1978 and requires only employers with 20 or more employees to include in such statements any disciplinary rules applicable to employees, and to indicate to whom they should apply if they are dissatisfied with any disciplinary decisions. The statement should explain any further steps which exist in any procedure for dealing with disciplinary decisions or grievances. The employer may satisfy these requirements by referring the employees to a reasonably accessible document which provides the necessary information. Section 13 is likely to come into force in February 1990. Prior to the 1989 Act all employers were required to include a note on discipline, regardless of the number of employed.

4 The importance of disciplinary rules and procedures has also been recognized by the law relating to dismissals, since the grounds for dismissal and the way in which the dismissal has been handled can be challenged before an Industrial Tribunal.* Where either of these is found by a tribunal to have been unfair the employer may be ordered to reinstate or re-engage the employees concerned and may be liable to pay compensation to them.

*Section 67(2) of the Employment (Consolidation) Act 1978 specifies that a complaint of unfair dismissal has to be presented to an Industrial Tribunal before the end of the 3-month period beginning with the effective date of termination.

Formulating policy

5 Management is responsible for maintaining discipline within the organization and for ensuring that there are adequate disciplinary rules and procedures. The initiative for establishing these will normally lie with management. However, if they are to be fully effective the rules and procedures need to be accepted as reasonable both by those who are to be covered by them and by those who operate them. Management should therefore aim to secure the involvement of employees and all levels of management when formulating new or revising existing rules and procedures. In the light of particular circumstances in different companies and industries trade union officials* may or may not wish to participate in the formulation of the rules but they should participate fully with management in agreeing the procedural arrangements which will apply to their members and in seeing that these arrangements are used consistently and fairly.

*Throughout this Code, trade union official has the meaning assigned to it by S.30(1) of the Trade Union and Labour Relations Act 1974 and means, broadly, officers of the union, its branches and sections, and anyone else, including fellow employees, appointed or elected under the union's rule to represent members.

Rules

6 It is unlikely that any set of disciplinary rules can cover all circumstances that may arise: moreover the rules required will vary according to particular circumstances such as the type of work, working conditions and size of establishment. When drawing up rules the aim should be to specify clearly and concisely those necessary for the efficient and safe performance of work

76

and for the maintenance of satisfactory relations within the workforce and between employers and management. Rules should not be so general as to be meaningless.

7   Rules should be readily available and management should make every effort to ensure that employees know and understand them. This may be best achieved by giving every employee a copy of the rules and by explaining them orally. In the case of new employees this should form part of an induction programme.

8   Employees should be made aware of the likely consequences of breaking rules and in particular they should be given a clear indication of the type of conduct which may warrant summary dismissal.

Essential features of disciplinary procedures

9   Disciplinary procedures should not be viewed primarily as a means of imposing sanctions. They should also be designed to emphasize and encourage improvements in individual conduct.

10   Disciplinary procedures should:

a Be in writing.
b Specify to whom they apply.
c Provide for matters to be dealt with quickly.
d Indicate the disciplinary actions which may be taken.
e Specify the levels of management which have the authority to take the various forms of disciplinary action, ensuring that immediate superiors do not normally have the power to dismiss without reference to senior management.
f Provide for individuals to be informed of the complaints against them and to be given an opportunity to state their case before decisions are reached.
g Give individuals the right to be accompanied by a trade union representative or by a fellow employee of their choice.
h Ensure that, except for gross misconduct, no employees are dismissed for first breach of discipline.
i Ensure that disciplinary action is not taken until the case has been carefully investigated.
j Ensure that individuals are given an explanation for any penalty imposed.
k Provide a right of appeal and specify the procedure to be followed.

The procedure in action

11   When a disciplinary matter arises, the first line manager or manager should first establish the facts promptly before recollections fade, taking into account the statements of any available witnesses. In serious cases consideration should be given to a brief period of suspension while the case is investigated and this suspension should be with pay. Before a decision is made or penalty imposed the individual should be interviewed and given the opportunity to state his or her case and should be advised of any rights under the procedure, including the right to be accompanied.

77

12   Often first line managers will give informal oral warnings for the purpose of improving conduct when employees commit minor infringements of the established standards of conduct. However, where the facts of a case appear to call for disciplinary action, other than summary dismissal, the following procedure should normally be observed:

    a   In the case of minor offences the individual should be given a formal oral warning or if the issue is more serious, there should be a written warning setting out the nature of the offence and the likely consequences of further offences. In either case the individual should be advised that the warning constitutes the first formal stage of the procedure.

    b   Further misconduct might warrant a final written warning which should contain a statement that any recurrence would lead to suspension or dismissal or some other penalty, as the case may be.

    c   The final step might be disciplinary transfer, or disciplinary suspension without pay (but only if these are allowed for by an express or implied condition of the contract of employment), or dismissal, according to the nature of the misconduct. Special consideration should be given before imposing disciplinary suspension without pay and it should not normally be for a prolonged period.

13   Except in the event of an oral warning, details of any disciplinary action should be given in writing to the employee and if desired to his or her representative. At the same time the employee should be told of any right of appeal, how to make it and to whom.

14   When determining the disciplinary action to be taken the first line manager or manager should bear in mind the need to satisfy the test of reasonableness in all the circumstances. So far as possible, account should be taken of the employee's record and any other relevant factors.

15   Special consideration should be given to the way in which disciplinary procedures are to operate in exceptional circumstances. For example:

    a   **Employees to whom the full procedure is not immediately available.** Special provisions may have to be made for the handling of disciplinary matters among nightshift workers, workers in isolated locations or depots or others who may pose particular problems for example because no one is present with the necessary authority to take disciplinary action or no trade union representative is immediately available.

    b   **Trade union officials.** Disciplinary action against a trade union official can lead to a serious dispute if it is seen as an attack on the union's functions. Although normal disciplinary standards should apply to their conduct as employees, no disciplinary action beyond an oral warning should be taken until the circumstances of the case have been discussed with a senior trade union representative or full-time official.

    c   **Criminal offences outside employment.** These should not be treated as automatic reasons for dismissal regardless of whether the offence has any relevance to the duties of the individual as an employee. The main considerations should be whether the offence is one that makes the individual unsuitable for his or her type of work or unacceptable to other employees. Employees should not be dismissed solely because a charge against them is pending or because they are absent through having been remanded in custody.

Appeals

16 Grievance procedures are sometimes used for dealing with disciplinary appeals though it is normally more appropriate to keep the two kinds of procedure separate since the disciplinary issues are in general best resolved within the organization and need to be dealt with more speedily than others. The external stages of a grievance procedure may however be the appropriate machinery for dealing with appeals against disciplinary action where a final decision within the organization is contested or where the matter becomes a collective issue between management and a trade union.

17 Independent arbitration is sometimes an appropriate means of resolving disciplinary issues. Where the parties concerned agree, it may constitute the final stage of procedure.

Records

18 Records should be kept, detailing the nature of any breach of disciplinary rules, the action taken and the reasons for it, whether an appeal was lodged, its outcome and any subsequent developments. These records should be carefully safeguarded and kept confidential.

19 Except in agreed special circumstances breaches of disciplinary rules should be disregarded after a specified period of satisfactory conduct.

Further action

20 Rules and procedures should be reviewed periodically in the light of any developments in employment legislation or industrial practice and, if necessary, revised in order to ensure their continuing relevance and effectiveness. Any amendments and additional rules imposing new obligations should be introduced only after reasonable notice has been given to all employees and, where appropriate, their representatives have been informed.

The following example of a disciplinary procedure is taken with permission from *Discipline at Work – The ACAS Advisory Handbook*.

DISCIPLINARY PROCEDURE

(1) Purpose and scope

This procedure is designed to help and encourage all employees to achieve and maintain standards of conduct, attendance and job performance. The company rules (a copy of which is displayed in the office) and this procedure apply to all employees. The aim is to ensure consistent and fair treatment for all.

(2) Principles

a) No disciplinary action will be taken against an employee until the case has been fully investigated.

79

b) At every stage in the procedure the employee will be advised of the nature of the complaint against him or her and will be given the opportunity to state his or her case before any decision is made.

c) At all stages the employee will have the right to be accompanied by a shop steward, employee representative or work colleague during the disciplinary interview.

d) No employee will be dismissed for the first breach of discipline except in the case of gross misconduct when the penalty will be dismissal without notice or payment in lieu of notice.

e) An employee will have the right to appeal against any disciplinary penalty imposed.

f) The procedure may be implemented at any stage if the employee's alleged misconduct warrants such action.

(3) The Procedure

Minor faults will be dealt with informally but where the matter is more serious the following procedure will be used:

Stage 1 – Oral warning

If conduct or performance does not meet acceptable standards the employee will normally be given a formal **oral warning**. He or she will be advised of the reason for the warning, that it is the first stage of the disciplinary procedure and of his or her right of appeal. A brief note of the oral warning will be kept but will be spent after . . . months, subject to satisfactory conduct and performance.

Stage 2 – Written warning

If the offence is a serious one, or if a further offence occurs, a **written warning** will be given to the employee by the first line manager. This will give details of the complaint, the improvement required and the timescale. It will warn that action under Stage 3 will be considered if there is no satisfactory improvement and will advise of the right of appeal. A copy of this written warning will be kept by the first line manager but it will be disregarded for disciplinary purposes after . . . months subject to satisfactory conduct and performance.

Stage 3 – Final written warning or disciplinary suspension

If there is still a failure to improve and conduct or performance is still unsatisfactory, or if the misconduct is sufficiently serious to warrant only one written warning but insufficiently serious to justify dismissal (in effect both first and final written warning), a **final written warning** will normally be given to the employee. This will give details of the complaint, will warn that dismissal will result if there is no satisfactory improvement and will advise of the right of appeal. A copy of this final written warning will be kept by the first line manager but it will be spent after . . . months (in exceptional cases the period may be longer) subject to satisfactory conduct and performance.

Alternatively, consideration will be given to imposing a penalty of a disciplinary suspension without pay for up to a maximum of five working days.

80

Stage 4 – Dismissal

If conduct or performance is still unsatisfactory and the employee still fails to reach the prescribed standards, **dismissal** will normally result. Only the appropriate senior manager can take the decision to dismiss. The employee will be provided, as soon as reasonably practicable, with written reasons for dismissal, the date on which employment will terminate and the right of appeal.

(4)   Gross Misconduct

The following list provides examples of offences which are normally regarded as gross misconduct:

– theft, fraud, deliberate falsification of records
– fighting, assault on another person
– deliberate damage to company property
– serious incapability through alcohol or being under the influence of illegal drugs
– serious negligence which causes unacceptable loss, damage or injury
– serious acts of insubordination
– unauthorized entry to computer records.

If you are accused of an act of gross misconduct, you may be suspended from work on full pay, normally for no more than five working days, while the company investigates the alleged offence. If, on completion of the investigation and the full disciplinary procedure, the company is satisfied that gross misconduct has occurred, the result will normally be summary dismissal without notice or payment in lieu of notice.

(5)   Appeals

An employee who wishes to appeal against a disciplinary decision should inform . . . within two working days. The senior manager will hear all appeals and his/her decision is final. At the appeal any disciplinary penalty imposed will be reviewed but cannot be increased.

Extension 3   The Department for Education and Employment booklet PL958 *Maternity Rights – A Guide for Employers and Employees* is available free of charge. Tel: 01709 888688.

Extension 4   The Department for Education and Employment booklet ITL 1 *Industrial Tribunal Procedure* gives further details. This can be obtained by calling the DfEE on 0171 925 5555. The address is: Sanctuary Buildings, Great Smith Street, London SW1P 3BT.

Extension 5   If you wish to attend an Industrial Tribunal as an observer, you should contact the Office of Industrial Tribunals – you should be able to find the address in the telephone directory. If in difficulty, contact ACAS on 0171 396 5100.

These Extensions can be taken up via your NEBS Management Centre. They will either have them or will arrange that you have access to them. However, it may be more convenient to check out the materials with your personnel or training people at work – they may well give you access. There are other good reasons for approaching your own people; for example, they will become aware of your interest and you can involve them in your development.

4 Answers to self-assessment questions

Self-assessment 1 on page 9

1 Yes. A contract of employment exists as soon as someone has accepted the terms and conditions of employment that they are offered.

2 All employees are entitled to get a statement, which spells out the main terms and conditions of their employment, within **two months** of starting work.

3 Once an employee agrees to the terms in a contract of employment, he or she must abide by them, or be guilty of **a breach of contract**.

4 As an employee, you are obliged to take reasonable care in the way you do your job, even if it doesn't say so in your contract. This is an **implied term** in your contract.

5 If a contract of employment incorporates a collective bargaining agreement, the terms of the contract can be changed without the express approval of the employee. This is known as an **incorporated** term.

6 A **breach of contract** occurs when an employer changes the terms of a contract without the consent of the other.

Self-assessment 2 on page 19

1 The main function of trade unions is to represent its members to management at all levels.

2 Collective bargaining is a process whereby unions negotiate with employers on behalf of all of their members in a particular organization.

3 When a trade union is granted **recognition rights** by an employer it gains the right to negotiate on behalf of its members, to receive certain kinds of information about the organization where it is organized, and to be consulted over redundancies.

When a union is granted **representation rights** it gains the right to represent individuals in cases of discipline and grievance.

4 The statement that 'Shop stewards are full-time union officials' is the only one that is not true.

Self-assessment 3 on page 52

1   All disciplinary offences involve a **breach of the rules**.

2   If a disciplinary offence is minor, a first line manager might decide that, rather than beginning the formal disciplinary procedure, they should have an **informal discussio**n with the team member.

3   **Everybody involved** benefits from there being clear rules for dealing with disciplinary offences.

4   Here are the actions you might take, set out in order.

    e   Decide who should be present.
    b   Decide where the meeting is to be held.
    f   Introduce the participants, and state why they are there.
    i   Give the employee a chance to state his or her case.
    a   Decide what penalty should be imposed.
    h   Sum up what's been said.
    d   Continue to monitor performance.

Self-assessment 4 on page 62

1   There are five grounds for dismissing someone fairly:

■ because of the employee's **misconduct**;
■ because of the employee's lack of **capability** or **qualification**;
■ **redundancy**;
■ a reason related to **the law**;
■ some other **substantial** reason.

2   A woman who has been on **maternity leave** normally has the right to her old job back.

3   An employee can claim unfair dismissal by resigning and then going to an Industrial Tribunal within three months.

4   A person must have been employed for two years before they can claim unfair dismissal.

5   Reinstatement means putting someone back in their old job without loss of continuity of employment. Re-engagement means giving the employee a different position within the company.

5 Answers to activities

Activity 23 on page 32

If you glance back through the procedure, you will see that the correct answers are:

1   Would every minor offence have to be taken through the procedure above? No: as is stated at the start, minor faults are dealt with informally.

2   In which stages do the warnings given become spent or are disregarded after a certain period of time? Stages 1, 2 and 3.

3 After which stages does the employee have a right of appeal? **All** stages.

4 At which stages are the warnings written down? **All** stages.

5 At which stages does the employee receive a written document? Stages 2, 3 and 4.

Activity 26
on page 35

1 **Mrs Jones in the wages department**

It might be difficult convincing someone that this was a disciplinary offence. Some of the reasons are that:

■ her office first line manager knew what was going on;
■ she took as little time as possible – using some of her coffee break;
■ other people had done the same thing, so there was a precedent;
■ her personal circumstances provided a good reason why she wanted to make the collection;
■ she made sure her work was done.

2 **Mrs Jones in the reception area**

You may agree that her behaviour warrants some form of disciplinary action. Some of the reasons you may have put down are that :

■ there is no evidence that she asked anyone's permission;
■ she spent a long time on the collection;
■ she had already been warned about her behaviour;
■ the collection could almost be considered as being for her own benefit;
■ it is part of her job to be in a specific place. In this case, it is important that somebody is there to meet visitors at reception.

If you agreed with my arguments, perhaps you will also agree that these two cases contrasted dramatically. One was clearly not an offence, while the other clearly was. If you have had experience of dealing with disciplinary matters, you will know that decisions are often much more difficult than this.

Activity 31
on page 47

The only answer to this question is: the procedure of the organization where you work.

If there is no agreed procedure, you could follow the example procedure given by ACAS (which you'll find reproduced in Extension 2 of this workbook on page 75). Obviously, any previous offences still on record involving the **same individual** may well affect your decision. Don't forget also that any previous cases involving **different** individuals but the **same offence** should be taken into account: the aim is consistency.

Activity 33
on page 48

You may have noticed a number of ways in which this ending of the interview is an improvement on our last example. The first line manager:

- stated what the offence was;
- gave Ray a chance to comment;
- gave the trade union representative the chance to comment;
- told Ray about the company's disciplinary procedure, and what a further offence might lead to;
- told Ray about his right of appeal;
- told Ray that the offence could be erased from the records after six months;
- made clear, unambiguous statements.

6 Answers to the quick quiz

Answer 1   You could have mentioned: the employer's name; the place of work and the address of the employer; the employee's name; the date employment began; the date on which the employee's period of continuous employment began; where the period is not permanent, the period it is expected to continue; where the employment is for a fixed term, the date when it is to end; the job title; the amount of pay and the interval between payments; hours of work; holiday pay and entitlement; sickness and sick pay arrangements; pensions; whether a contracting out certificate under the Social Security Act 1975 is in force; notice periods; a note specifying any disciplinary rules and to whom employees can apply if they are dissatisfied with a disciplinary decision; a note on grievance procedures specifying to whom employees can apply to seek redress of any grievance; any collective agreements which directly affect the terms and conditions; where a person is required to work outside the UK for more than one month, the period he/she is to do so; the terms and conditions relating to his/her return to the UK.

Answer 2   These are terms that are too obvious to mention, or which are not stated because they are accepted custom and practice in the kind of work being done.

Answer 3   Some implied obligations are: to exercise reasonable skill and care in doing your job; to be honest in your dealings with people; to take care of an employer's property; to be loyal to your employer (such as refusing to provide a competitor with company confidential information); to obey reasonable instructions.

Answer 4   Statutory terms are those imposed by law.

Answer 5   The levels are: the union branch level; an intermediate level; the delegate conference.

Answer 6   A shop steward is: an employee, with a job to do; a representative of the individual in discussions with management about grievances and so on; a representative of a group in collective negotiations.

Answer 7   A collective bargaining arrangement is a procedure whereby employers and employee representatives agree to negotiate matters, such as pay and conditions of service, on a group basis for the employees in a particular company or industry.

Answer 8   Discipline at work has the four main objectives of: safety; prosperity of the organization; fairness; compliance with a contract.

Answer 9   You should have mentioned: new employees; people who don't speak English as their first language; young people.

Answer 10   Stage 1: oral warning. Stage 2 – Written warning. Stage 3 – Final written warning or disciplinary suspension. Stage 4 – Dismissal.

Answer 11   ACAS suggest that gross misconduct includes: theft, fraud or deliberate falsification of records; fighting, or assault on another person; deliberate damage to company property; serious incapability through alcohol or being under the influence of illegal drugs; serious negligence which causes unacceptable loss, damage or injury; serious acts of insubordination.

Answer 12   We said that the purposes of a disciplinary interview are to:

- allow the employee to give his or her version of the incident;
- ensure a full discussion, so that everyone present has a chance to hear the facts and to present any new facts;
- advise the employee of his or her rights;
- enable a fair judgement to be made so that an appropriate penalty can be awarded.

Answer 13   The reasons are: because of the employee's misconduct; because of the employee's lack of capability or qualification; redundancy; a reason related to the law; some other substantial reason.

Answer 14   To earn the right to claim for unfair dismissal, an employee, whether employed full-time or part-time, must have completed two years' continuous employment with this employer.

Answer 15   This can happen when the employee resigns because the employer has broken the contract and/or has acted in a very unreasonable manner by treating the employee unfairly in some way or other.

7 Certificate

Completion of this certificate by an authorized person shows that you have worked through all the parts of this workbook and satisfactorily completed the assessments. The certificate provides a record of what you have done that may be used for exemptions or as evidence of prior learning against other nationally certificated qualifications.

Pergamon Open Learning and NEBS Management are always keen to refine and improve their products. One of the key sources of information to help this process are people who have just used the product. If you have any information or views, good or bad, please pass these on.

NEBS MANAGEMENT DEVELOPMENT

SUPER SERIES

THIRD EDITION

Managing Lawfully
– People and Employment

....

has satisfactorily completed this workbook

Name of signatory ....

Position ....

Signature ....

Date ....

Official stamp

SUPER SERIES

SUPER SERIES 3

0-7506-3362-X   Full Set of Workbooks, User Guide and Support Guide

A. Managing Activities

B. Managing Resources

C. Managing People

D. Managing Information

SUPER SERIES 3 USER GUIDE + SUPPORT GUIDE

SUPER SERIES 3 CASSETTE TITLES

To Order - phone us direct for prices and availability details
(please quote ISBNs when ordering)
College orders: 01865 314333 • Account holders: 01865 314301
Individual purchases: 01865 314627 (please have credit card details ready)